The Man Who Changed His Skin

Also by Thomas Fensch ...

The Man Who Was Dr. Seuss:
    The Life and Work of Theodor Geisel

The Man Who Was Walter Mitty:
    The Life and Work of James Thurber

    and ...

Steinbeck and Covici:
    The Story of a Friendship

Conversations with John Steinbeck

Essential Elements of Steinbeck

The FBI Files on John Steinbeck

Conversations with James Thurber

Of Sneetches and Whos and the Good Dr. Seuss:
    Essays on the Life and Work of Theodor Geisel

Behind Islands in the Stream:
    Hemingway, Cuba, the FBI and the crook factory

Oskar Schindler and His List:
    The Man, the Book, the Film, the Holocaust
    and Its Survivors

The Kennedy-Khrushchev Letters

Life, Love, Losses and Dogs:
    A Memoir with Paw Prints

    ... and others

The Man Who Changed His Skin

The Life and Work of
John Howard Griffin

Thomas Fensch

New Century Books

ISBN hardcover: 978-0-9832296-0-5
ISBN paperback: 978-0-9832296-1-2

New Century Books
P.O. Box 186
Ashland, Va., 23005-0186

NEWCENTBKS@GMAIL.COM

Cover photograph of John Howard Griffin by Father George
Curtsinger, reprinted with permission of the Curtsinger
estate.

Typesetting by Jill Ronsley, Sun Editing & Book Design,
suneditwrite.com

Contents

Acknowledgments

THE AUTHOR WISHES to thank the following for their help and counsel during the completion of this book:

Robert Bonazzi, for his permission to use text and photographs of John Howard Griffin and his help answering questions about Griffin's life and times;

Dr. Claude G. Perkins, President, Dr. W. Franklin Evans, Vice President, and Dr. Vincent Mumford, Associate Vice President, of Virginia Union University, Richmond, for providing research funds to make the completion of this book possible;

Ms. Tara Craig and her colleagues in the Rare Book and Manuscript Collections, Columbia University Libraries, New York, for her help obtaining material from the Griffin archives at Columbia.

Chronology:
Key Dates in the Life of
John Howard Griffin

1920   Griffin is born June 16, in Dallas, Texas and raised in Fort Worth.

1935-1939   Not yet 16, Griffin journeys to France for a better education that he could get in Texas. He studies medicine and music. When World War Two breaks out, he joins the French Underground as a medic and smuggles French, German and Austrian Jews away from the Nazis. His name is eventually on Nazi death lists and he is sought by the Gestapo. He escapes to England, to Ireland and back to the U.S. in 1940. His experiences form the basis for his first novel, *The Devil Rides Outside*.

1941-1945   He joins the Army Air Force and serves in the South Pacific for 39 months, one year of that time with a tribe of aborigines on a remote island; that experience was the basis for his second novel, *Nuni*. His vision is damaged by a Japanese air attack on Morotai. He is discharged, and returns to Texas, where a diagnosis of eventual blindness is confirmed.

1946   He moves again to France to spend his remaining sighted time in study. His eyesight deteriorates steadily.

1947   He returns to Texas blind, in the early summer of 1947 and is completely blind until January, 1957.

1949   Griffin meets critic John Mason Brown, who encourages him to write about his experiences.

1951   Griffin converts to Roman Catholicism, July 12. He eventually becomes a Third Order Carmelite; a married layman who can participate in the sacraments.

1952   His first novel, *The Devil Rides Outside*, is published; Griffin wrote it while he was blind.

1953   June 2. Griffin marries Elizabeth Ann "Piedy" Holland.

1956   His second novel *Nuni*, is published. He also wrote it while he was blind. *The Devil Rides Outside* is judged pornographic in Detroit; that decision was upheld by the Michigan Supreme Court.

1957   His eyesight returns, unexpectedly. He sees his wife and his two children for the first time. (They eventually have two more children.) The U.S. Supreme Court decides that *The Devil Rides Outside* was not pornographic, which was hailed as a major victory for authors, publishers, librarians, booksellers, and readers.

1959   *Land of the High Sky* is published, his first book after his eyesight returned.

1959   October 28. His first diary entry for *Black Like Me*.

1960   August 17. Last diary entry for *Black Like Me*. Griffin and his family move to Mexico in August, 1960 to escape death threats in Texas. Griffin returns to his interest in photography, which he had begun in France prior to World War Two. He becomes widely known for his portrait and scenic photography; all his photographs were taken only with available light. He and his family are eventually forced to leave Mexico by a regional revolution of Mexican Communists. They return to Fort Worth in May, 1961.

1961   *Black Like Me* is published. The hardcover edition sells 100,000 copies. The subsequent U.S. paperback edition sells five million copies during the decade of the 1960s. It was published in England, France, Germany, Italy, Holland and sixty other countries throughout the world, in thirteen languages, selling ten million copies worldwide.

1963   Receives the Pacem in Terris Award, named after a 1963 encyclical letter by Pope John XIII that calls upon all people of the good will to secure peace among all nations. *Pacem in Terris* is Latin for "Peace on Earth." Griffin shared the award that year with President John Kennedy.

1968   *The John Howard Griffin Reader* is published.

1969   *The Church and the Black Man* is published. Griffin becomes the official biographer of Thomas Merton. He works on a Merton biography for nearly the next decade.

1970   *A Hidden Wholeness: The Visual World of Thomas Merton* is published.

1973   *Twelve Photographic Portraits* is published.

1974   *Jacques Maritain: Homage in Words and Pictures* is published.

1975   Griffin is savagely beaten by the Klu Klux Klan in Mississippi and left for dead. He sustains permanent kidney damage.

1977   *A Time To Be Human* is published. He is unable to complete the Merton biography because of advanced diabetes and is forced to use crutches or a wheelchair. The Merton project is turned over to another writer.

1978   He begins to have a series of heart attacks; his health begins to deteriorate.

1979   One leg has to be amputated because of diabetes.

1980   Griffin continues to have a series of heart attacks. He dies September 9, of a cerebral hemorrhage, at 60.

1981   *The Hermitage Journals* is published.

1983   *Follow the Ecstasy: The Hermitage Years of Thomas Merton* is published.

1997   *Encounters with the Other: A Personal Journey* is published.

2003   *Street of the Seven Angels* is published, a novel he also wrote while he was blind.

2004   *Scattered Shadows: a Memoir of Blindness and Vision* is published.

2008   *Available Light: Exile in Mexico* is published.

2011   *Black Like Me* has been in print for fifty years.

a caveat to the reader ...

IN ADDITION TO his published books, articles and essays, John Howard Griffin kept a journal from 1950 to 1980, which ran to more than 3,000 single-spaced pages. Some of his journal entries became raw material for his published works.

He was an exceptional witness to his own life.

The author has made every effort to allow Griffin to speak through these pages, to tell his remarkable life story in his own words.

Readers will find material from Griffin's books, articles and other material set separately on the page, as well as material from his friends and colleagues. It would be a disservice—an injustice, in fact—to render his voice still, when there is so much material extant on Griffin's life, his contemporaries and those times.

I have fought the good fight,
I have finished the race,
I have kept the faith ...

—2 Timothy 4

Prologue

JOHN HOWARD GRIFFIN was once told "now you go into oblivion."

John Howard Griffin was always going into oblivion.

He was, in the title of Robert Heinlein's science fiction classic, "a stranger in a strange land."

He was always a stranger in strange lands. Multiple strange lands. Locales he steered himself into—to investigate—to go into oblivion.

And by accident of war—he encountered a world for ten years he could not possibly have predicted—or imagined.

Or returned from.

One of his favorite words was *strange*.

One |

France

The Devil Rides Outside

1935
Tours, France

JOHN HOWARD GRIFFIN, not yet sixteen, travels by
himself from his native Texas to France.

Griffin was always autodidactic. His mother Lena ...
had studied to be a concert pianist and gave piano lessons. His parents raised four children but only he had
learned what his mother knew about music. At four-
teen, he read of pianist Moritz Rosenthal, an eminent
musician with degrees in medicine and philosophy;
Griffin had found a role model, who "opened me up to a
far more fascinating horizon." At fifteen, frustrated by
the regressive public school system, he spotted an ad-
vertisement for a lycée, (a French school that prepared
students for university), a boy's school in France and
wrote a letter pleading for admittance.

Over four decades later, he remembered those days:

> My father was a man that I will never understand. He was from Georgia. He was brought up in that fundamentalist religion which said that anything remotely pleasurable was sin. He set aside Sundays as a particularly sober time. He was brought up in an incredibly racist atmosphere. But he never implanted any of those ideas in me. My dad was a kind of miracle, a matter of pure grace. He was a wholly decent, uncorrupted human being.
>
> It was a horrendous sacrifice on his part to send me to a French lycée at such a young age. In those days, we didn't even have air mail. It was the belief in the south that France was utterly immoral and Catholic. They didn't know which was worse.
>
> I had what they used to call a photographic memory. I could memorize a whole school course in one week. I was bored out of my mind, so they sent me to France, because in French schools you could advance as fast as you could learn. Also, there was a medical scholarship, and I was utterly impassioned by the sciences.

He sailed to France in search of an education he clearly could not receive in Fort Worth, Texas in the 1930s. He was admitted to the Lycée Descartes in Tours (learning French in the process and presumably some Latin as well, to study medieval Gregorian chants) and, after graduation, obtained a scholarship to the University of Poitiers (branch at Tours) where he took literature courses. He also studied medicine at the School of Medicine of Tours. During his second year of pre-med., he also worked at the Asylum of Tours.

Medicine and music became his twin passions; both can be seen in obvious and more subtle ways in his early books.

He became an assistant to Dr. Pierre Fromenty, director of the Asylum of Tours. One of Fromenty's psychiatric techniques was to treat with, or at least expose psychiatric patients to, the soothing qualities of Gregorian chants. Griffin became fascinated by these techniques. At the same time, he was studying music with Father Pierre Froger, an organist at Tours Cathedral. Griffin and Froger even co-authored a scholarly paper on music, *Interpretation of the Ornaments of the Music for Keyboard Instruments of the 17th and 18th Centuries*, privately published in 1939.

But World War Two changed everything.

Fromenty was drafted into the French Army and left and Griffin found himself in charge of 120 patients in the Asylum of Tours.

At nineteen, Griffin became an active member of the French Underground.

Griffin remembered:

> I had worked in France smuggling Jewish people out of Germany until France fell. I was (then) twenty, a research assistant at the Asylum of Tours. When the war came, they conscripted all the doctors and medical students into the service. They couldn't conscript me because I was an American citizen. I was immediately ordered back to the U.S. I refused to go because France had formed me. How can I flee at this time of need?
>
> I was put in charge of the asylum. Then I got involved with the French underground,

smuggling Jews out of Germany, across France, into England. We would use asylum ambulances, put our refugees in straitjackets and move them that way. They didn't have to speak. Many of them didn't speak French. They didn't have safe-conduct papers, of course. We didn't know how to steal, we didn't know how to forge (documents). We were infants in this, but we did the best we could.

He and others moved German, Austrian and French Jews to safety.

The Nazis were moving in. I will be haunted to my death by those scenes. We brought the people inside these rooms and kept them hidden. We had to tell the parents who had children under fifteen that we weren't going to make it. Suddenly I experienced a double reality. The first: a parent said "It's all over for us. Take our children." We would move anybody under fifteen without papers. You sat there and realized these parents were giving their children away to strangers. The second: I could go downstairs into the streets and find perfectly good men who went right on rationalizing racism ...

Finally Tours was over-run by the Nazis. Plans made by the French underground were discovered by the Nazis. Before the time his Texas boyhood friends may have been celebrating their twenty-first birthdays, Griffin's name was on Nazi death lists and he was actively pursued by the Gestapo.

When one of his student friends was shot by the Gestapo, Griffin was forced to go into hiding.

"Having witnessed the tragic effects of the Holocaust, refined to hideous perfection by the Nazis, he never forgot the horror," Robert Bonazzi wrote in the Introduction to *Scattered Shadows*.

This encounter with anti-Semitism may well have been one of the motivations for *Black Like Me*, decades later.

He was soon smuggled out of France to England, to Ireland then to the United States.

Griffin returned to France in 1946, first to Fontainbleau, to study music with Nadia Boulanger French composer, conductor and music professor (1887-1979). Griffin had hoped to become a composer. He was in good company. Among her other students had been Leonard Bernstein and Aaron Copland. He also studied with the French pianist and composer Robert Casadesus, whom he had met previously in Tours.

From Fontainbleau he moved to Paris, where he spent some time in a monastery, until he was cleared to study at the Abbey of Solesmes, the monastery where the original Gregorian chants are catalogued in the *Paleographie Musicale*, and study with the Benedictine monks, the world's foremost musicologists of medieval plainsong. He had first wanted to be a composer, but eventually decided to become a musicologist specializing in Gregorian chants.

Life in a French monastery was grueling: daily rituals of meditation, prayers, mass and chores; living conditions were no more advanced than during medieval centuries. Eventually Griffin could no longer continue at Solesmes; his health became very much at risk in primitive monastic conditions.

Griffin had met the theater critic John Mason Brown in 1949 and Brown suggested that Griffin write about his experiences.

His monastic life in France gave him his first book, *The Devil Rides Outside*.

It is a first-person novel-cum-memoir of an American who travels to France to study medieval musicology. The novel's focus, or fulcrum, is of the interior of the monastery, with lives devoted to Christ, rituals, masses, meditation and spartan life, contrasted with carnal life outside the walls. The title is an old French proverb "La diable rôde autour d'un monastére"—"the devil rides outside monastery walls."

Griffin spoke the text of the novel into a wire recorder (in French) at night and then transcribed the tapes (into English) onto a typewriter the next day. The first draft of the novel was competed in within seven weeks, although it was revised several times over the next two years. The eventual first hardcover edition was 596 pages.

The Devil Rides Outside has a musical foundation, which may not be apparent to casual readers; Griffin based it on the form, or structure, of Beethoven's *String Quartet Opus 131*.

It was not only Griffin's first book; it was the first book of a new publishing company, Smiths, Inc., established by two brothers, Gordon and J. Hulbert Smith in Fort Worth.

It was a surprising success; *The Devil Rides Outside* was chosen as a selection of the Book of the Month Club.

Critic Clifton "Kip" Fadiman wrote the review which appeared in Book of the Month Club flyers. Some of his review appeared on the back jacket of the hardcover edition of *The Devil Rides Outside*:

> A staggering novel, this, in its length, its faults, and its qualities.... the hero is a young American.... He comes to a Benedictine monastery, somewhere in the north of France, to study manuscripts of Gregorian chant. The diary of his experiences there and in the neighboring village forms the narrative. At bottom this is a psychological confession-novel turning on the most potent of all themes—the struggle within a single human soul between God, of which the monastery brothers are an emblem, and the devil, symbolized by the sensual temptations held out by the village plus the bias toward the flesh within the narrator himself. At the start he is a non-believer; but after ... intense soul-searching, arguments with the monks, and sexual experiences described in torrid ... detail, he is at last driven, rather than led, to spiritual peace. Mr. Griffin's ... intense psychological analyses ... recall Dostoyevsky or Pascal. The pure doctrine of asceticism has rarely been so effectively demonstrated in twentieth-century fiction. The whole book is a kind of modern *Temptation of St. Antony*, without Flaubert's controlled art, but also without its frigidity. Mr. Griffin's baroque excesses are easy to ridicule, but—at least to this reviewer—they seem the excesses of an intense temperament and possibly of a notable literary talent.

Early in the book, Griffin reveals this as a *roman a cléf*; the unnamed first-person narrator is Griffin's alter ego.

(The fictional Father Clement is based on Griffin's real mentor Friar Andre Hussar, who also had to be smuggled away from the Nazis when Griffin was forced to leave. Hussar's brother Jean later returned, joined the Free French Army and was killed in a firefight with the Germans. Jean was Griffin's best friend in Tours):

> We talk of my trip to the monastery, of our interests in art and music, and of my background, first as a medical student and later as a musicologist. He draws me out until I become conscious that for one of the few times in my life, I am talking freely and with complete honestly. Instinctive realization that there's no need to exaggerate here, no need to cover one's faults. Father Clement talks easily and intelligently as a man. He is particularly interested to know of my life as a medical student. And when he prepares to leave, much later, my impatience is largely gone. As he shakes my hand, I ask him about their life. What makes a man embrace such a life? How can they accomplish what they do living under such a rigid schedule?
>
> "You will need to understand these things gradually, my son," he laughs. "Tonight I will leave you some books. You may stay up as late as you like. Do you have everything? What about cigarettes?"

And Griffin's protagonist reveals Griffin's continuing interest in medicine, when he is implored to save the life of a village child dying of untreated, or untreatable, epilepsy:

"What is it, Jacques? If I can be of any help—?"

"The Chevissiers—you know, the family who work our farm—their little daughter is ill. I think she's dying, but they refuse to spend a penny to call a doctor. Could you look at the child? You told me you've been a medical student."

"But, Jacques, I'm no doctor. I never got beyond pre-medical work."

Griffin's narrator is unable to affect any cure for the child:

A gasp from the child as her left arm jerks into the air, to fall half-back and be pulled up again on some drunken, invisible senseless string. Arms and legs tremble, slowly at first as in some macabre dance, becoming more frenzied gradually until the even rattle of her breathing grows labored, until the viscid mucus foams from her nose in gray bubbles to burst on the air. Her head moves slightly from side to side with great rapidity. Repeated short gasps come from her lips as we watch. The climax will take her. We know it but we work doggedly, hoping always that she may dance it out and still live. I heat the pads on her head and throat, wiping dampness from her colorless straw hair with a towel. Emaciated child against the strength of death. The dance continues.

The child is beyond help and does die. The narrator is furious that the parents never called a doctor sooner. Then he realizes that village gossips may well accuse him of letting the child die, gossip which he believes will eventually happen, perhaps more sooner than later.

The narrator encounters monastic life far more primitive then he expects; no heat in the monastery, food little better than gruel, few comforts of any kind. Eventually he moves to a flat in the nearby village and journeys to the monastery library daily. In the carnal world of the village, he has a one-night affair with a French woman, then agonizes that she might be ostracized by other village women and driven from the village.

The female owner of the flat he rents at first appears to be polite and cordial, but eventually becomes—in his eyes—an absolute shrew.

Throughout the novel are extensive passages of theological debate between Griffin's unnamed protagonist and various Catholic monks. These passages may be more significant to Roman Catholic readers or, at least, deeply spiritual readers.

As Clifton Fadiman rightly observed in his review for the Book of the Month Club publicity, "he is at least driven, rather than led, to spiritual peace."

> Monastic formality gives way to brief visits from many of the monks. There is a loneliness of rain and somberness within, that makes us feel the fringes of night during the day. Father G'seau knocks on the open door and bows his smiling way in, followed shortly by father Dutfoy. We talk of the monastic life and its history. Father Dutfoy, who is from the Midi, constantly mentions the tropics. He is always wiping his brow, on which there is only imaginary perspiration, and sighing, "Oh, how I should love to live in those places—and to be warm again."

The books come, are read and digested, and replaced by other books. The spell of the monastery begins to enter my blood, and the years of study in the outside world grow more remote. The reasons for the monastic life become more apparent as time passes. but a man is unable to live this way unless he believes, with St. Benedict, that God makes suffer only those whom He loves. For in his *Regula* Benedict states that we must not only accept all hardships; and that above all we must never "murmur" against anything which arises in our monastic life, as such discontented murmuring is a sin. To live like this under the stringent vows of a monk, requires either a religious vocation of the highest order, or an interest, such I have, in research. And yet I know that no amount of interest can give me the strength to continue this life for long ...

... he continues to wrestle with his own soul ...

"There, Father," I break in, "that's what I don't get, that's the reason I can't stand these books of piety. They're full of such dogmatic phrases—God's love, the devil's evil, and all that muck."

Father Clement looks at me.

"It is a good sign to see you like this, my son," he remarks very quietly. "If you were sure of your own disbelief, our beliefs would not annoy you. It is because you became uncertain that you are troubled. Is that not it?"

"I guess so"—disconsolately—"but I never accept."

"Will you let me say something that may appear very naive to you?"

"Say anything you like."

"Do not fight so hard to hold on. The moment the devil sees a sign of belief, he causes that belief to become so painful to you that you are in reality suffering from the devil, and not from God. Know that you are not essentially different than any of us here. None of us is struck, none of us is 'enlightened.' We struggle, and sometimes we lose. Few men have an unquestioning vocation. Like you, we are filled, day by day, with unremitting temptation."

It does not become any easier for Griffin's narrator ...

"My God, my God, forgive me. Forgive me and have mercy upon me. Make me love Thee, make me love Thee despite myself. Force me, I beg Thee to want *THY love.*" I lie in my prayer, but the words come, and I cringe from them. "Make me want Thee above all other things. Forgive me my coldness. Let me learn the impossible grace; a faith, a belief, a love which is pure; a love which asks no questions, which expresses no doubts. Let me know why these other things are wrong, why they are really wrong. Let me, O God ..."

The prayer dies in my throat with the chill—suddenly—as I wonder to what I have been praying.

I waste my breath seeking an image that is false. No, no, they say it is real; it has to be real. But the doubt is there, and I cheapen myself and become a fake. I pray to a wall in which I have no belief because I think it may warm my belly with some trifling goodness of feelings. I utter idiotic prayers to a darkened vein of the soul.

Torn between the carnal and the chaste, the village outside the Benedictine Monastery overwhelms him. Griffin's alter ego nearly loses his moral and spiritual bearings; he discovers it is impossible to bridge the two worlds, physically so near and spiritually so distant. Ultimately, he makes a decision, however reluctantly:

> My sigh rasps loudly in the silence. Words seem to formulate themselves, sounding heavy and automatic. "Can I come back here, Father?"
> "Do you really want to, my child?"
> "Yes, I say tiredly. "I think I almost have to, now. I can't go on—" I shrug my shoulders and look at him.
> "I know, my son." He touches my arm again. "Yes, by all means come back if it means that much to you. You may have your old cell this Sunday. I will help you move in."
> "Thanks Father." I turn to go, but falter. "Just one thing more, Father. You knew all this—why didn't you tell me sooner?"
> "You had to come to it yourself, my son...."

The Devil Rides Outside is clearly an anachronism; as Clifton Fadiman observed, more closely related to Dostoyevsky, Pascal and Flaubert than to other contemporary twentieth-century novels.

Griffin subsequently said the novel "wrote me into the church." He was baptized as a Roman Catholic July 12, 1951, (before the book was published) even though it is far from clear that Griffin's alter ego in the novel is totally converted.

And only the readers who saw Griffin's photograph on the back jacket of the hardcover edition ever guessed what an achievement that book was for Griffin.

Two |

The South Pacific

Nuni

World War Two
The Solomon Islands and Morotai

GRIFFIN FLED THE Gestapo, fled France, to England
to Ireland and then to the United States. In 1941, he
enlisted in the Army Air Force, at the time when the
Army and the Air Force were not yet separate. After
basic training, he was sent to the South Pacific as an
intelligence officer/language expert.

Griffin spent 1943 living in a native village on a remote island in the Solomon chain, assigned to study the
indigenous culture, translate the dialect of the inhabit-
ants, and gather strategic information on Japanese positions from the native allies. At first he viewed them as
"primitives"—as *Other*.

But after he was unable to navigate jungle trails
without a five-year old boy to guide him, it became obvious "that within the context of that culture, I was
clearly the inferior—as an adult man who could not have

survived without the guidance of a child," he admitted, Robert Bonazzi wrote in the Introduction to *Scattered Shadows*.

Griffin was able to chart the language of this tribe phonetically. The analysis of this dialect would place him in the Florida or Nggela islands, just north of Guadalcanal. His chart still exists: the following was marked in pen -ORIGINAL- in the top right corner of the first page. This is part of his translations of the oral dialect:

VIA NAMBETI QUEENO	(VIA NAM-BETI QUEE-NO)	I WANT A DRINK.
ELEONGUNA	('LÈON-GU-NA NA-EEN)	I WANT A DRINK.
ALOGO BETI VIM	('LOGO BETI VI˘M)	DO YOU HAVE WATER IN THE HOUSE?
MAI QUEENU	(MY QOO-EE-NOO)	GIVE ME WATER.

INAU VITE	(EENA-OO VITAY)	I AM HUNGRY.
I NAU VANGATI	(VA-NGA-TI)	I AM EATING.
IGANI CORNI	(I-GAN-I COR-NI)	I EAT CORNI (CORN).
ELEONGUNA CORNI		I SHOULD LIKE SOME CORN.

While living with Pacific islanders, Griffin developed a friendship with John Vutha, Grand Chief of the Solomons, who was a staunch alley of the Americans in battling against Japan's occupation. Vutha provided crucial information by tracking enemy movements and, when he had been captured and tortured by the Japanese, he refused to divulge allied positions. After 22 bayonet wounds, they left him for dead, hanging from a tree as an example. "There is little doubt that if he had given in and spoken," Griffin writes, "the American victory at Guadalcanal would have been much slower in coming. Countless lives would certainly have been lost that were saved by his silence." For his heroism, Vutha received the highest awards accorded by the British and American governments.

... Griffin biographer Robert Bonazzi later wrote.

Grand Chief Vutha united all the Solomon Islands tribes before the Japanese invasion. Griffin not only knew Vutha, but also "married" a native South Pacific island tribal woman, in a ceremony traditional to the Solomon Islands. When Griffin began studying to become a convert to Catholicism, he told his spiritual advisor, Father Langenhorst, who decided that the marriage would not be considered "binding" in the Catholic church. Griffin did not mention this Solomon Island ceremony in any of his writings; Bonazzi only heard about it years later, from Griffin's wife Elizabeth.

His experiences on the island led to his second novel, *Nuni*, eventually published in 1956. Griffin translates *Nuni* as *World*. He had a "next work" clause in his contract with Smiths, Inc., obligating him to offer that publishing firm his next project after *The Devil Rides Outside*. But on the strength of his Book of the Month Club success with *The Devil Rides Outside*, he was able to move to the mainstream publisher Houghton Mifflin. Smiths had become inactive as a publisher by the time

Nuni was ready. The main title page reads: "Published by Houghton Mifflin Company, Boston, in association with Smiths Inc., Dallas, Texas."

The Devil Rides Outside and *Nuni* share three characteristics: both are first-person narratives. The narrator is never given a name in *The Devil Rides Outside*; in *Nuni* his name is mentioned only twice—John Harper, literature professor.

Both have musical motifs as foundation: Beethoven's *String Quartet Opus 131* in *The Devil Rides Outside*; the antiphonal structure form of the Gregorian Chant in *Nuni* and both have anecdotes showing Griffin's passion with medicine.

Robert Bonazzi writes that "while the first novel builds a bridge towards a religious conversion, the second maps paths of physical pain, emotional loss and spiritual crisis—Harper's and Griffin's."

Nuni is a modern Robinson Crusoe, Daniel Defoe's 1719 novel of a castaway who spends 28 years on a remote tropical island near Venezuela.

Griffin's John Harper is the sole survivor of an airliner disaster; he washes up on the shore of an un-named island and barely survives his ordeal. Eventually he meets a native tribe, begins to communicate by drawing symbols with a stick in the sand and eventually learns their language.

"John Harper is symbolic of modernity-as-useless to one stripped of civilized trappings," Bonazzi writes.

Harper eventually meet a prepubescent native girl:

> "Do you want a name?" I tease, feeling authority and liberation return to my stunted bloods.

Her eyes open in blank surprise and her head starts forward in a movement of expectancy.

"Since you are no bigger than a finger, I name you Ririkinger."

Her hand flies up to my chest. I sense its faint weight through the thick mat of my beard.

"'Kinger?" she whispers.

"You," I say solemnly, "are not N'gari kikiki daoka. You are Ririkinger."

"'Kinger! 'Kinger! 'Kinger," she laughs.

The *ger* syllable in *Ririkinger* seems oddly jarring as it is not even remotely close to the rest of the native dialogue in *Nuni*.

The native world of John Harper's tropical island is full of hearing, smelling, tasting and touching sensations.

Eventually Harper discovers that Ririkinger must undergo a coming-of-age face-marking ritual, so horrific it might kill her. He steals her away and inadvertently kills an ancient crone, the village matriarch, in the progress. Harper and Ririkinger escape.

Griffin's Gregorian chant motif appears toward the end of the novel, as a series of stream-of-conscience passages, variations on a single theme:

Standing alone at the edge of the compound, looking at these sodden huts, a phrase haunts my brain in repeated chantings:

driven along paths not of their own choosing

What are they?—these beings that surround me with their sleeping. How is it they seem so dead and yet so move my affections, bound up

as they are in the paraphernalia of snoring and
flesh and hungers and salivas and hairs?
  driven along paths not of their own choosing
Affection excites my heat with answers that
cannot be formulated by the brain, truths from
some far memory of the soul; intimate truths
forever strangers to the intellect, truths stem-
ming from:
  driven along paths not of their own choosing

Griffin uses that phrase 19 times in 12 pages.

Readers might anticipate a resolution toward the
end of the novel; a glint of metal in the sky, a seaplane
gliding to a stop, a lone figure striding onto shore, like
MacArthur returning to the Philippines or a lone figure
crashing through the jungle with machete in hand and
a hearty—"We finally found you ..."

There is no such denouement; no such resolution.
John Harper has saved Ririkinger from the face-marking ritual; but he has also lost much of his memory of
civilization and of time. He no longer knows whether a
specific day is Thursday or Sunday, although he writes
those words in the sand. There is virtually no hint that
he might ever return to civilization.

After Griffin's success with *The Devil Rides Outside*,
Nuni was also judged exceptional, and he was compared
(by more than one critic) to William Faulkner.

In 1956, an evaluation of Griffin's career by Lon
Tinkle, appeared in *The Dallas Morning News*. Tinkle
had a very lengthy career as critic. His essay/review is
worth reprinting in full:

'Nuni': Faith Beneath the Form

The keyboard of John Howard Griffin's talents and soul has a range and depth not common in Texas writing. More than a lyric cry or a nostalgic recall or a tribal legend, his work has the rich texture and diversity of a symphony.

His first novel, "The Devil Rides Outside," was a shattering experience. Internationally acclaimed for its originally and vitality, the novel presented powerfully Griffin's own spiritual evolution, from a simple delight in the flesh to a religious respect for man's infinite complexity. His novel dramatized the conflict between man's animal and his angel self in one brilliant tableau after another.

Though the setting of Griffin's new and second novel, "Nuni," is a far cry from the provincial and monastery France of his first book, its theme is identical.

Strictly speaking, the new novel is not a novel at all—it is a rhapsodic poem, an allegory really, of man's struggle to fulfill himself in the largest sense that religious faith allows. It is a large sense with Griffin, who, like Graham Greene and Mauriac and Faulkner and other thoughtful novelists of our time, is dedicated to renovating the spirit and faith beneath the form.

But don't go away yet. Griffin is a novelist of ideas, yes, and of the fundamental ideas, but he is also an artist.

He uses a drama to exploit his purpose—but still it is drama.

"Nuni" draws, as did "The Devil Rides Outside," on the author's personal experience.

Like the first novel—it is a scrupulous testimony to what Griffin has observed in a highly specialized community.

* * *

This time the community—a far cry from the French monastery town of the first book— is an island of primitive savages in the South Seas. (Griffin, as a language specialist, performed a mission for the army in World War II on Guadalcanal.)

The governing factor in the daily life of these loveless, joyless and brutal primitives is the inherited set of taboos.

Taboo has become for them, a slavery. Far from leading the carefree and easeful joyous lives of the South Pacific myth, these naives are mere mechanisms "driven along paths not of their own choosing."

They have been deadened, through the power of unexamined tradition, into an animality as little aware, as little purposeful, as little vital, as that of a beaten ox. The whiplash in their case is the ritual of taboo, which puts them at the mercy of ignorance, superstition and hatred.

* * *

With shock, this is the truth discovered by the book's narrator, a professor in his fifties who survives a plane wreck at sea when he alone of he passengers is washed afloat on the island shores.

What this civilized twentieth-century man finds immediately unbelievable is the natives' hatred of sex. He soon discovers why. Fear and ignorance cause the males to believe that mating means self-destruction; the girls, through superstitious error, share in this reduction of love to mere biology.

As the American learns to survive their hostility and as he manages to endure, he makes one discovery after another. He finds total indifference to the notion of parenthood; in short, a life that represents no more than blind Elemental Nature.

When a winning little child is about to be needlessly sacrificed in a crazy initation rite, the American finally intervenes. The credit he has established through his American know-how (a few simple cures of simple ailments) gives him enough prestige to make his lesson to the natives palatable. His lesson is that humanity is, in a sense, anti-destiny.

We can and will choose our lot, through the religious principle of love freely given. The book closes with the missionary outlook of this South Sea island, at least, a whole universe away from the uncomprehending puritans of Somerset Maugham's "Rain."

But before the end, Harper sees that only the tiniest gap separates civilization from the automaton primitive. Over here, we too suffer from mechanization, taboo, curdled forms, joylessness.

In two ringing, beautifully written and keenly thought sections, thinker Griffin takes over and writes a powerful essay on the nature of love and a scathing condemnation of modern values. Both are organized in fugal form, orchestrated like rich music. And why not? Like music, they bespeak intimate truths, "beyond the demand of intellect."

* * *

In brief, the narrator here accepts dualism, a division of body and spirit; but he believes in man's greatness because of our god-given responsibility, of free choice, of self-realization. Whether from primitive stupidity or wrathful morality, any stifling of man's freedom diminishes his worth and returns him to slavery.

"Nuni" is a serious work from an impassioned mind. It is uneven, demanding, sometimes over-written. But it is a solid achievement that guarantees faith in Griffin's immensely meaningful future.

Tinkle's essay/review is part insightful criticism, part adulation, part hyperbole. Griffin, after all, was a native Texan, who lived within the circulation area of *The Dallas Morning News;* it was well known that he hit the Book of the Month Club with his first book and of course, when *Nuni* was published, it was also well known he served in the South Pacific during World War II.

"Uneven, demanding and sometimes over-written" could also describe *The Devil Rides Outside,* as well.

Griffin spent one year on the remote island then was assigned to the landing base on Morotai. Japanese invasion plans had been intercepted. Much later, he remembered the those days in the South Pacific:

By 1945, we had lost so many men and had been bombed so often that we had long ago learned to refuse any thoughts about death. Death did not exist for us except as a cold fact to be recognized and quickly dismissed. We had long ceased to mourn the deaths of our companions.

In life, a warm and often devoted friendship existed between us. In death, nothing. They were there at the table one day, and then we saw them no more and that was all.

Most of us in the 425th Bomb Squadron's radar section were in our third year overseas. Although our unit had been bombed often, this was the first time we were under a black alert. Now we were threatened with invasion from the enemy. We stood, perhaps a dozen of us, in the radar tent on Morotai Island and drew straws. Pops Fendler drew first, and then Mills. Each got a long straw. I was third in line and got the short one. Corporal Fred Kaplan cast me a glance of sympathy, tossed the remaining straws into the coral dust at our feet, and cursed.

The section captain told me I would go on duty at six this evening.

"Do you know what to do?" he asked.

"Not entirely."

He glanced up at the tent roof where rot holes let in thin rays of sunlight. "Intelligence has intercepted the Jap's orders. They are supposed to take the airstrip, kill the tower operators, and then proceed here to the radar tent, kill whoever is on duty, and take all our technical data before it can be destroyed. You'll have to have your gasoline ready to burn the place up. And you'll have the jeep outside to make a run for it. If they follow orders, they'll hit the tower first and you'll have some warning."

"The camp area had been evacuated when we reached our tents. Morotai had quickly become a ghost island. Rumors spread that the Japanese has massed a force of 47,000 men across the bay, while our total remaining American and Australian forces were about a tenth of that.

Griffin took a jeep to his assignment, a radar tent:

Then the high, uneven rumble of airplane motors, emerged from the silence. Hearing the "Washing Machine Charlies," as we called the Japanese bombers.... The motors drone louder, many of them.

Then I began to trot down the slope away from the radar tent toward a trench shelter we had long ago dug.

A massive pattern bombing began at the far end of the strip. I judged they were dropping one hundred pound bombs every twenty-five yards.

A spotlight caught one of them and other spots raked across the sky to converge on it from all angles and follow its flight. Anti-aircraft guns boomed and red splotches exploded high in the air around the bomber. The tiny fleck of silver did not swerve from its course.

As the bombers approached, I coldly concentrated on their height and the angle of the bombs' descent. Beneath me, as though detached from the upper body, my legs moved like pistons carrying me rapidly over the coral. A shell shrieked downward and I threw myself to the ground.

Covering my head with my hands, I heard my voice boom back from the wet coral against my face—*Mater misericordiae*. While I cringed against the falling bomb, I felt astonishment that these words had burst into consciousness.

The shell exploded nearby and shrapnel whizzed unseen around my body. Relief and exhaustion overwhelmed the senses. The soaked ground chilled through my shirt and coral granules gritted between my teeth. I wanted to lie still and rest, to ignore some gigantic urgency in the atmosphere. Then a new wave of motors, ack-ack explosions, and shell screeches swept toward me. I hurried to my feet to run ahead of it.

The black edge of a ravine we used for an ammunitions dump brought me to a halt. I realized I had missed our bomb shelter by a hundred yards or more. I turned to go around the ravine, listening always to the planes and the pattern of explosions. Then I headed on at the exact angle.

If it dropped its bombs they would pulverize me. I heard the high starting screech and felt intestines convulse. For an instant, I stood paralyzed, listening to the bombs hurtle toward me. Without any voluntary movement of my own, I felt my body hurl itself over the cliff and crash into the ravine.

Two days later when I regained consciousness, I lay naked on a bed.

Griffin had sustained a severe concussion, permanent loss of some memory and his vision had been damaged....

Three |

Darkness

The secret behind The Devil Rides Outside and Nuni ...

1947
Texas

... JOHN HOWARD GRIFFIN was blind.

His blindness did not happen when he awakened two days later, hospitalized from the horrific Japanese bombing. It did not happen a week after that, or two weeks later, but Griffin did become blind.

He had been in the Army for more than four years; in the Pacific three years and three months. He was sent back to the states, to a mustering-out center near San Francisco. Griffin passed all the final physical tests, except for one; the vision test. He was told he had 20/200 vision.

I was stupefied. I felt I could see reasonably well and yet 20/200 meant that I could see at 20 feet what a person with normal vision would see at 200 feet. I was legally blind.

At the same time Griffin was told he had 20/200 vision, he witnessed an incident which, in a variety of circumstances, was being repeated again and again throughout the country:

We continued through a series of interminable lines. Standing in the sunlight, I saw a tall, heavily decorated black sergeant who was being berated by the young white corporal who had charge of getting our group into the proper lines.

"You may be a damned hero overseas, but you're nothing but a nigger here—and don't you forget it."

I approached the gathering group.

The sergeant, his body in a violent tremble, whispered: "I've been four years fighting for this mother-fucking country, I'm damned if I am coming back to this shit."

"You're back in it alright," the corporal shouted back.

The armed forces were not fully integrated until 1948 by President Harry S. Truman and the segregationist Jim Crow laws were not broken until the Supreme Court decision Brown v. Board of Education in 1954.

Did Griffin store this incident away in the catacombs of his memory, as genesis for *Black Like Me*?

Griffin returned to Texas where the diagnosis was confirmed by a neurosurgeon—his eyesight had become so inadequate, the neurosurgeon suggested that Griffin should give up the idea of a career in medicine. Griffin resolved to return to France and spend his remaining sighted months in study.

He *had* been to France—studying the calming effects of Gregorian chants among psychiatric patients with Dr. Fromenty and studying music with Father Pierre Froger. And studying medicine, at least as far as pre-med. He wanted to return and spend his remaining sighted months in France, where he had lived before the South Pacific, before the remote island, before Morotai, before the Japanese bombing, before traveling back to Texas.

He returned to Fountainebleau in the summer of 1946, and he began a deeply spiritual transformation:

> I feared myself—feared that I would not be able to cope with the temptation to play the tragic figure, to become the noble sufferer accepting the world's pity.
>
> I knew that my fiercest struggles would not be against losing sight, but against the assaults of public opinion about blindness that would judge my condition tragic.
>
> Faced with nothing, very little becomes everything.

His declining vision was also accompanied by horrific headaches.

He eventually entered the Benedictine Convent of St. Jacques, to a world of routine little changed since the middle ages or before. It nurtured his soul yet surprised him, at the same time.

> I soon perceived that my stay would not be
> a matter of instruction. No one would seek to
> guide me in anything. I was left alone to absorb
> what I could from the atmosphere, from the
> rhythms of monastic life and from the liturgy.
> All needs were cared for.
>
> My deepest bewilderment—and edification—
> lay in finding that all my preconceptions of
> monastic formation were utterly false. I had
> imagined that men seeking union with God
> languished in a state of mystical trauma,
> soaring above the baser aspects of daily living.
> But here men lived in intimacy with the rich
> polyphony of philosophy and theology rather
> than with some lyrical emotionalism. The odors
> of cabbages and mop water no longer jarred
> against the fragrance of incense, but were
> complementary.

And he had long philosophical conversations with his mentor Friar Hussar, fictionalized in *The Devil Rides Outside* as Father Clement.

The horrific headaches became more frequent and his vision became increasingly blurry.

He journeyed to Tours, where he had lived in his previous sojourn in France. And Griffin met a blind man, a bookseller on the streets of Tours. "The Blind Man of Tours" became an integral part of his transformation and Griffin's essay by that name became one of his most famous publications of that period of his life. Griffin became curious how a blind man could sell books on the street; how he would know the titles and how he could accept the correct payment for his books.

Griffin found the man's flat; he wanted to know what it was like to be blind and, at first, the blind man was taken aback by Griffin's questions. The man had jazz playing in the background:

> "You didn't come for a book, though, did you?"
>
> "No sir."
>
> "Did you come to see a blind man?" He asked and leaned forward, his face covering my entire field of vision, consuming me.
>
> "Yes sir ..."
>
> The jazz raked across us.
>
> "Why?" his voice exploded, as though he dreaded the answer.
>
> I wished for silence. The room needed silence. But we were bombarded by the cheap upsurge of saxophones and clarinets.
>
> "Because I had hoped to learn something from you ..."
>
> "From me?" he said in sneering disbelief. "What, for example?"
>
> "How you do things. How you live. What it's like ..."

When Griffin admitted that he was going blind, he saw a look of stunned anguish on the man's face. The blind man of Tours began to teach Griffin what he could.... Griffin offered to a buy a book—*any book*, Griffin thought. At the end of an exceptional evening, Griffin forgot to take a book along. And then he realized that he never knew the man's name—and the Blind Man of Tours never knew his name.

Griffin moved to the Abbey of Saint Pierre of Solesmes, living in a cell like any other monk. The stay would be all too brief. The Abbey was heated little better than during the middle ages. In December, 1946, Griffin contracted malaria. He lay burning with fever in a freezing cell at the monastery. He fell unconscious.

The fevers recurred so frequently that by January, 1947, he had to leave the Abbey. He simply could not withstand the constant cold and was not able to gain strength on the meager diet which sustained the monks. He rented a villa nearby (which presumably became the source of the interior scenes in *The Devil Rides Outside*) and trekked back and forth to the Abbey. He found if he wrote with a pen, he could see the lines only as a blur.

In the spring of 1947, at 27, John Howard Griffin became completely blind.

At that point, the overhead globe (of a light) appeared to him like candlelight seen through dense fog. And he continued to wrestle with ... with every aspect of blindness:

> I knew that those I loved would suffer far more than I would suffer. I carried the responsibility not only of accepting what came, but also comforting them. And the best way to comfort them was to nullify the stereotypes of blindness, to work for skills that would dispel sadness and make them forget my condition. and even as I realized this, I was certain it was beyond my own capacities. I saw the enormity of the task and saw it would require help.
>
> I must be in perfect, voluntary obedience to a greater force, do out of obedience what I could

not do from my own imperfect initiative. There
was suddenly no alternative. If others were to
be spared, I must make the last act of will....

He went to the chapel and may have silently said *le
grand oui* ...

> I forced the words out. The *Great Yes*. If
> you exist, take me for what I am. I hold noth-
> ing back. Show me what you want me to do. I'll
> obey no matter how repulsive it is to me person-
> ally. I give you myself totally and without any
> reservation.

And still navigating each day constantly presented
challenges:

> When I tried to eat, either I speared my lip
> with the fork or the food dropped into my lap.
> When I reached for a glass, I often knocked it
> over. I lost my direction in the middle of the
> room and had to walk until I bumped into a wall
> to locate myself.
> My nerves jangled with each unexpected
> noise. I found myself cursing in solitude, trem-
> bling with impotent rage. The reality of blind-
> ness presented a thousand roadblocks alto-
> gether different from those I had attempted to
> foresee. I was thankful to have this initiation
> alone, to make the mistakes unobserved. How
> did a man comb his hair or find his clothes or
> shave? And what did he do during the hours ex-
> cept sit and wait for someone to come and take
> his arm and lead him somewhere.

He discovered an old monk who was also blind. The monk offered wisdom from his decades of blindness:

> Learn to reach for a glass properly. Do it five hundred times and you'll never knock one over. Get yourself a lightweight fork and then you can tell by the weight if you bring it to your mouth empty or if it had food on it. You are a musician. You have already learned that a passage of music you cannot play the first time comes easily into your hands after practicing it twenty or a hundred times. I still learn this way. I am amazed all the time how quickly things come, and I've been without my sight for many years now, maybe twenty.

Every part of daily life posed a problem. How would he even urinate without making a mess? The old monk told him: learn to straddle a commode so he was touching it with the insides of both legs, then aim down between his legs.

Griffin wanted to shake his hand in friendship. But how? The old blind monk suddenly snapped his fingers, Griffin reached out to the sound and they shook hands.

He took a ship home and on board met a doctor from Guatemala. They spoke French together and Griffin received yet another lesson, a lesson from the doctor in musical terms he clearly appreciated:

> "There are two main activities for you now.
> "First there is the activity that do not involve seeing at all, like listening to the radio or a concert or lying awake in the dark. They are consonant situations.

"However, if you were at a sporting event, you would be acutely aware of your lack of sight. That would be a dissonant situation."

"Yes, that make perfect sense," I said. Since the doctor was making a psychological distinction using a musical metaphor and I was a musician who had studied medicine, what he said struck with precision.

"Each of us must find some way to balance out the psychologically dissonant situations with consonant situations that allow tensions to resolve," he continued, "or else your nervous systems collapse eventually. Now, without your sight, you still must live in a sighted world. You face many dissonant situations that people with sight are spared. Some of these will change into consonant situations as you learn to solve your problems and handle yourself better. Until you learn the skills you will need, it seems to me that you just have to avoid too many dissonant situations, or at least take time to recuperate from them by seeking consonant situations deliberately."

Griffin returned home; his parents had always wanted to move to the country, so they had bought a farm outside Mansfield, Texas, 20 miles south of Fort Worth.

Griffin had to face the fear of failure, to face the "paralysis of caution," to venture, to take a step, to *do*. Every step, every activity was a challenge to overcome, especially outside the farmhouse:

I fell into gullies, walked into low-hanging tree limbs, got lost. It was worth the falls to kill the fear. To gain maximum freedom, my parents would frequently go into town. With the certainty no one watched, I began to develop astonishing speed, even running along pathways in the woods. I soon discovered I could locate myself by the feel of the terrain under my feet, by the sunlight on my face, by the direction of the wind.

And Griffin simply refused to become a *victim*. Or a curiosity.

> To most sighted people, blindness is simply the worst tragedy that can befall a man. The world tells you in a thousand ways that you are a pitiful figure. Few believe that you can be happy and interpret your own natural happiness as stoicism or bravery. To have people constantly whispering how pathetic you are becomes a grinding irritation. ... Most blind persons neither want pity for their "misfortune" nor applause for the simplest accomplishment.

He journeyed into Fort Worth, to the Lighthouse for the Blind. He "learned all the Brailles."

He learned to raise livestock and bought chickens and Poland China hogs. He would feed, and judge them by feel:

> I felt no loss of dignity when I sat in a farrowing pen in the middle of the night to help a sow farrow her pigs, drying them with a tow sack, clipping their umbilical cords and notching their ears before returning them. On the contrary, I felt satisfaction in doing it, or raking

stockpens or plucking the geese for down or rendering lard in a huge iron kettle over a wood fire. I found a parallel between the farm life and what I had loved at the abbey of Solesmes. In both instances, in relative isolation and close to nature. I lived a simple, uncomplicated life. The liturgy, the chants, the silence were carried within when I worked. As it had been in France, so it was on the farm. Values held important by sighted society were supremely unimportant to me. I lived not behind cloister walls marked by bells but by the hunger of stock animals, by the woods in all their seasons and by the cycle of birth and death in nature.

He entered livestock competition, under a different name, so no one could claim he had an advantage because he was blind. He had stock shown in the Southwestern Exposition and Fat Stock Show in Fort Worth, and won prizes for his Poland China hogs.

He also raised Toulouse geese and Golden Roller canaries.

Other ranchers accepted him as an equal; he once overheard someone say "you don't need to feel sorry for him. He can do as good without his sight as the rest of us can with ours. He sure takes all the prizes.'"

He enjoyed the company of the other stockmen; after daily competition, they would go out to eat and play cards. None of them would play poker with him if he used a deck of Braille cards. They feared he could read their own cards with his fingers as he dealt them. He couldn't do that, but he never told them so.

He learned to walk with a cane and he gave lectures on musicology to area colleges and universities.

In 1949, he went on a concert tour with Robert Casadesus, whom he had met previously in France. The tour began in Dallas, where he met professor and book critic Lon Tinkle; they conversed in French together and they subsequently became life-long friends. In New Orleans, he met Sadie Jacobs, who had been blind since three. She taught Griffin how to navigate the world. He learned to use a flexible white cane, instead of a heavy one he had used previously. He learned to walk through the streets of New Orleans by himself:

> She opened up a new world to me.
>
> Perhaps most importantly of all, she taught me to get rid of the "blind look." The sightless rarely look toward the person speaking to them. Like most, I tended to keep my head rigid and hold it too high, as if I was staring at the skies. The blind do this unconsciously. In some circles, it is brutally but accurately termed "the dumb look."
>
> "Aim your face directly at the speaker's voice," she instructed. "Animate your face. Show expressions. Move your head frequently. Remember to them you are not only Howard Griffin, you are a symbol of all blind people in the world. They will judge others by you."
>
> Then she explained that "part of our problem now is that the sighted have seen too many beggars, too many ill-trained blind. So I want you to remember this: You will have succeeded only when you can make people forget you are blind."

Griffin, who went by the name John or Howard, took her advice; it was all part of his journey. He had been blind for two years when he met her. And when he returned to Texas, he met critic John Mason Brown, who urged him to become a writer. How? Griffin asked. "Get paper and a typewriter and begin," Brown said, simply. *Surely it couldn't be that easy*, Griffin thought, but he returned to the Lighthouse for the Blind in Fort Worth and asked for typing lessons. He began on a Thursday, on an old Underwood typewriter. By Monday he knew how to type "with fair facility."

His father helped convert a feed room of their barn into a studio. It was barely three steps in each direction. It may have occurred to Griffin that his studio was much the same size as the cells he lived in, while he was staying in the Benedictine monasteries in France, and used for much the same purposes—introspection and learning.

Griffin's ideas and words poured out, perhaps faster that he anticipated. It was an *epiphany*:

> Then the characters, who at first seemed dead, began to come to life and acting with a vitality of their own.
>
> I wondered if this might be my true vocation, so casually stumbled upon. All of past studies seemed to have been a preparation for these long days and nights when I poured out pages of a first novel.
>
> My past training in giving up something beyond myself tempered life now. I immersed my being in the atmosphere, in the movements, and in the characters. The process became more hypnotically real than anything else. Soon the work took over so completely that I moved a cot into the feed room and lived there night and day.

Griffin had to learn to judge his own sensibilities as a writer:

> Each time I came to a passage where a truth appeared in conflict with current standards of good taste, I would ask myself if it would offend God. I soon discovered to my considerable amusement that God would appear to be much less narrow-minded than those who pretended to act in His name.

His background in music sustained him—in fact, his knowledge of the forms of music supremely aided his work:

> In my first attempt at a novel, which became *The Devil Rides Outside*, I used the forms of Beethoven's *String Quartet Opus 131*, a work I knew intimately. The characters enter as Beethoven's themes enter and are developed in the same way. The novel's four principal female characters were created as the embodiments of four sensual types as the protagonist reacted to them. But I responded to them as representations of the four variations Beethoven had used in his quartet. When the theme of the novel did not match the music, I changed the novel.

Griffin wrote *The Devil Rides Outside* as a first-person narrative simply because that was the only technique he understood. He finished the novel in the summer of 1947 and immediately wrote *Handbook for Darkness*, a lengthy monologue/ guidebook for the blind and their families, friends and colleagues. It was published by The American Foundation for the Blind in print and Braille editions.

In his student days in Tours, he began keeping a journal; he now returned to it instinctively and discovered it greatly aided his work:

> A private journal—with no thought of anyone else seeing it—allows the writer to rip the dull curtain off his thoughts, to record feelings, problems, emotions, reactions, temptations, and all of the private dramas and dreams. Most importantly, it is a way to recall those ideas and scenes that will soon escape memory unless set down on paper. If honest, it will contain the tremendous advantage of giving him a truer self-knowledge, which can be horrifying, sometimes overwhelmingly so, for it is humbling to see oneself without illusions. But it is the best way to compassion and wisdom.
>
> The journal allows the writer to create directly and without wending his way through all the jungles of delusion and self-aggrandizement. The true writer, like the true painter, is an observer of all things, and quite especially of himself; but of himself in detachment, as though part of him stood away and appraised the rest, without love or partiality.

John Steinbeck used much the same method. Each day he wrote a journal/diary entry to "warm up" his pen—he wrote his novels in longhand because that method slowed down his writing and allowed him to concentrate on the flow and pace of his manuscript-in-progress. He kept a journal during the months he wrote

The *Grapes of Wrath*, published in 1939, and that journal has been published as *Working Days: The Journals of The Grapes of Wrath* (1989). And later, he used the same method when writing *East of Eden,* published in 1952. His *Journal of a Novel: The East of Eden Letters* has also been published (1969). Both books of his journals/diary entries offer substantial insights about how a novelist views himself and his craft and how he visualizes and articulates his work.

The Devil Rides Outside was published in the fall of 1952. When Smiths Inc. sent out review copies and publicity material, Griffin's secret was revealed.

Newspaper headlines from those days tell the story:

Blind War Veteran's Book
To Be Sent to 300 Reviewers

Blind Man Writes Way
Into Catholic Church

Blind Man's Book Draws Praise
From Nation's Literary Critics

Blind Author
Off to Consult
Literary Critics

Success for Blind Author

Novel Written in Barn at
Mansfield Praised Highly

An article by his friend Lon Tinkel, in *The Dallas Morning News* Sunday, Oct. 12, 1952 was headlined:

Writing Farmer of Tarrant County
Violates All 'Typical Texan' Rules

Readers outside the circulation areas of Texas newspapers knew nothing of this: outside of Texas, *only the readers who saw Griffin's photograph on the back jacket of the hardcover edition ever guessed what an achievement that book was for Griffin.*

On the back cover he is shown wearing black glasses, his chin resting on the curved handle of his white cane. Obviously blind.

Years later, he told Studs Terkel:

> I learned to type and wrote six books. They'd say, "You're extraordinary." I'd say I'm not. It's just that I refuse to let them put me into a cloistered workshop. I resent very deeply the underchallenging of the blind, the young, the black.

Six books. Written while he was blind. Or perhaps at least five. *The Devil Rides Outside* and *Nuni* were published during his lifetime. One other novel, *Street of the Seven Angels* was published posthumously. A fourth, *Passacaglia* remained unfinished. Another, apparently a comic novel based on his father-in-law, Clyde Parker Holland, was lost.

Griffin claimed six books; his literary executor, Robert Bonazzi, says he wrote five while blind. Griffin *did* have long-term memory loss from the bombing on

Morotai. Three have been published, one unfinished, one lost.

John Howard Griffin not only learned to adjust to his blindness, *he turned a handicap into enlightenment.*

Griffin's tropical world in *Nuni* is full of hearing, smelling, tasting and touching experiences precisely because Griffin was blind when he wrote it and he was concentrating on all the other senses except vision.

The Devil Rides Outside sold out the first printing of 5,000 copies and a second printing was scheduled by October 27, 1952.

But Griffin had other concerns—he had met Elizabeth Ann Holland. She was a music student, studying with Griffin's Mother. She was 17, he 32 and blind. But, as Griffin said:

> I had always been considered controversial, yet I felt not controversial at all. I was sightless but refused to live down to the sighted view that I was handicapped. I was a writer who refused to spin out popular books. If I allowed myself to become average—a totally dependent blind man or an unscrupulous writer—I could never be normal or live naturally. That was not bravery on my part, but simply survival.

He did not visualize himself as handicapped, neither did Elizabeth Ann Holland. They thought nothing of their age differences. They were married June 2, 1953 and honeymooned in Mexico City. His new in-laws gave them 24 acres and a cottage on the Holland farm. Griffin wrote all his fiction in the barn studio at his parent's farm.

Griffin began to experience medical problems, which would plague him throughout the rest of his life: first a rare type of diabetes, difficult to control, and tumors on his feet. He had to use a wheelchair. In May, 1954, he began to lose the use of his legs, due to damaged nerves at the base of his spine.

By July, 1954, a diagnosis was confirmed: he could hobble around slowly, but might become paralyzed. Griffin began to have deep doubts—why had he subjected Elizabeth Ann to a marriage to an older blind man, now barely able to walk?

Their marriage survived all of Griffin's medical crises points; they eventually had four children. The marriage was broken only by Griffin's death, in 1980.

Pocket Books printed a paperback edition of *The Devil Rides Outside* in 1954. Then it was censored in Detroit. It became a test case in obscenity. The Detroit ruling was based on a statue banning any book "containing obscene, immoral, lewd or lascivous language ... tending to incite minors to violence or immoral acts'"

The ban was appealed to the Michigan Supreme Court, where it was upheld.

"The ramifications of such a statue are staggering," Griffin said August 1, 1954, "because logically everything from the Bible to Shakespeare could be banned on this basis."

An Associated Press article distributed October 21, 1956, said, in part:

> "Some of the things I wrote in my novel made me sick to my stomach, but I had to write them to be honest.

"But honesty in depicting a character is one thing, while obscenity is another. The problem could be solved if there were a clear legal definition of obscenity."

The courts, Griffin said, have not come forward with an adequate definition so far, and he hopes the Supreme Court, ruling on his case later this year, will provide one.

Although Griffin expected a Supreme Court decision in 1956, it was not until February 26, 1957, that a unanimous ruling by the Supreme Court was announced. *The New York Times* carried a front-page headline:

High Court Voids Obscene Book Act

The Devil Rides Outside had been cleared of the charge it was pornographic. The landmark ruling, written by Justice Felix Frankfurter, established several significant points in favor of authors, publishers and booksellers. It stated that a book must not be judged pornographic on the basis of isolated passages taken out of of context, but the entire work must be taken into consideration. It directed all states to revamp existing statues on pornography, protecting booksellers from future illegal incursions and clarifying the censorship battleground nationwide.

And Frankfurter wrote,

It is clear on the record that appellant was convicted because Michigan made it an offense for him to make available to the general reading public a book that the trial judge found to have a potentially deleterious influence upon youth. The state insists that, by thus quarantining the

general reading public against books not too
rugged for grown men and women in order to
shield juvenile innocence, it is exercising its
power to promote the general welfare. Surely,
this is to burn the house down to toast the pig ...
The incidence of this enactment is to reduce the
adult population of Michigan to reading only
what is fit for children.

"A magnificent statement. How sweet is justice,"
Griffin said.

The Devil Rides Outside was not only a Book of
the Month alternate selection as his first novel, the
Supreme Court ruling following the censoring in Detroit
was a major victory for all writers, all publishers, all
booksellers, all libraries, all readers.

Elizabeth Ann had become pregnant; on November
20, 1954 they had their first child, a girl, Susan Michelle.

In 1956, he became involved in a desegregation crisis in the Mansfield, Texas public school system. He co-
wrote, with Theodore Freedman, of Houston, a lengthy
monograph, with "What Happened in Mansfield." It was
16 single-spaced pages, and was "based on a series of
interviews with residents of Mansfield and others directly connected with the local situation. Some of the
interviews were recorded directly, in other instances
the interviewer recorded his impressions immediately
after the interview." This encounter with segregation
in the public schools of his hometown must surely have,
again, reinforced his sense of injustice in the world.

In 1956, Griffin and Elizabeth had their second
child, a boy, Johnny.

And beginning in January, 1956 Griffin began using
two recording machines to complete *Nuni*—he transfered

spoken text from one, along with edited changes into the second. This, he said, speeded up the process and eliminated tedious re-typing.

> I had been very close to *Nuni*—aware perhaps that I had been putting the problems of my own life into the lap of Professor Harper, desperate for the narrator to solve them. I had stripped him of everything that men generally consider necessary to function at the human level—family, friends, even clothing—and plunged him into a world in which he was ill-prepared to live. My prospect was similar, though I never mentioned it out loud.

And, he later admitted, the tribal islanders he encountered in the South Pacific were far more humane than those he portrayed in *Nuni*.

When he finished the manuscript, Griffin faced the postpartum depression common to many authors when a major project is finished:

> Now it is gone. They are all gone, all of these characters who have been more real than many people I know during these past years. They walked out the door with stamps on them. Their existence disappears when words stiffen into print. The printed word is the tomb of human spoken utterance. The body of the speaker is elsewhere.

And on January 9, 1957, an unimaginable—a most remarkable—event occurred quite suddenly and unexpectedly ...

Four |

Darkness Visible

"... I thought I saw the back door, cut in portions, dancing at crazy angles."

January, 9, 1957
Mansfield, Texas

... JOHN HOWARD GRIFFIN could see. His vision came back.

Suddenly and unexpectedly, his eyesight came back, as he was walking from his barn studio to his parent's house to begin lunch....

> Redness swirled in front of my eyes. Then
> I thought I saw the back door, cut in portions,
> dancing at crazy angles.

Elements continued to dance and he had pain in his eyes and head.

Griffin's mental gyroscope, which had held him steady in the universe throughout the years, suddenly spun out of control.

He got to a telephone and called his wife. All he could say was, "I think ..."

"What is it?"

"I think I can see," he said and began weeping.

> I sat in the chair at the table. The room was broken up. Triangles of color faded and swirled. Weird designs of floor and wall and ceiling fused. It was like being hit a terrible blow on my head. My system could not bear the shock. Numbness filled me.
>
> Dimly I thought of all those sightless people who had for so long been my brothers and sister. Was I actually leaving their world, to which I had been so accustomed?
>
> I prayed for the presence of mind never to forget them, to do or say nothing that would build false hopes in them or hurt them. Was something happening to me that would never happen to them? Dear God, would this hurt them, would this make them feel more lonely? And I was concerned with my family. Was I really seeing? Would their hopes be built up ion to crash when this incredible storm passed?
>
> Another thought stuck me and almost twisted my brain. Was ever a man in a stranger position? My own wife and children, people who were my life, and yet if I saw them in the street I would not even know them! From the swirl of my own confusion, I thought of how my wife must feel. Should she run immediately to me?

Should she take time to dress, fix herself up, so
I could see her first in the best possible light?

The doctor arrived, but Griffin could not see him—
only a splotch of the blue in the corner. The doctor gave
Griffin a shot and talked, presumably to soothe him.

> I no longer remember the words, for my
> mind was blotting out, trying to become uncon-
> scious. I sat, holding myself up, drained of all
> strength, all intelligence. The sedative made
> me withdraw into a deep calm, far from myself.
> It closed out the world. I heard myself asking
> what the sedative was.

"Demerol, a light sedative. I want you to be aware of
everything. This is an experience few can have."

> My wife and children. Would I know them?
> Would I know my parents, after all these years?
> Strange and twisted perceptions came to mind.

Later a car pulled into the driveway. He heard its
door slam. Nerves simmered up from numbness. "Tell
me who it is," he said to the doctor.
"Your parents."

> I prayed vaguely and braced myself, prayed
> that this not be a deception for them. They had
> suffered too much, too gallantly on my account.
> Then there was a swirl of movement. Faces
> drew close to mine. They were kissing me, talk-
> ing in low tones. I had to pull out of it, to reas-
> sure them in some way.

"Can you actually see me?" my mother asked.
"I can see you have on a green dress." I mumbled.

I couldn't control the vision enough to see
their faces. I would see a portion of their clothes
and instantly the ceiling or a wall—then haze.

Talk went on around me. I retreated into a
stupor until the sound of another car aroused
me. I stayed seated at the table. At the door, I
heard the voices of my wife and children. I staggered up from the chair. Susan ran forward and
was the first to appear. I concentrated beyond
strength to see all the radiant wisdom of her
two-year-old face looking up at me.

"You beautiful little thing," I said, touching
her cheek.

I saw her face clearly then it blurred.

Suddenly, Elizabeth was in my arms, her
face beside mine. I glimpsed raven black hair.
Johnny was tugging at my pantslegs. I reached
down, felt his short-cropped hair, but could not
see him. The first clear view of my daughter
had been like looking at the sun, blinding me to
everything else. That image remained in front
of my face during the next dim hours. The effort of seeing her, or perhaps the emotion, had
shattered me.

The next day, the psychic overload continued:

There were reporters and photographers,
and the beginning of the nervous rigors that
shook the whole body. I concentrated on the
blind, knowing that I must say nothing to hurt
them or give them false hopes. I sat numb in
the eye of a hurricane of activity. But I had no

recollection of their questions or my answers. I was collapsing without realizing it.

The press loved the story, perhaps because it was an unexpected sequel to the blind man-writes-novel stories they had published previously:

‘Suddenly I Could See’:
Novelist Regains
Long-Lost Vision

Finally Sees Children
*Blind Author Regains
Sight After 10 Years*

… and even the next day:

The next morning I was having hard rigors. No recollection of that day. I was virtually unconscious, although I moved and spoke. I saw a hall full of reporters and photographers, and I think I said yes to everything they wanted, but remembered no specifics. The I was taken to the eye specialist. The press mob followed us. The specialist said he would have temporary glasses made immediately. My doctor was concerned about the pressure from the reporters and laid down the law.

No more interviews. But Griffin continued to be besieged by the press; he had to be smuggled out of the doctor’s office and home.

Senator Lyndon Johnson called, with a typical Johnsonian message: this was the only Texas miracle he could not take credit for.

The articles continued:

Author Still Glorying
In Restoration of Sight

His Sight's Restored,
He's Still Dumbfounded

*Griffin in Seclusion
To Avoid Pressures*

Even *Newsweek* and *Time* had brief articles about him: in the Newsweek column "Newsmakers," the third week in January, under the title "Sand and Sight" and *Time* magazine, in the issue dated Jan. 21, 1957, in the section, "Medicine," under a title "Second Sight."
Time wrote, in part:

Last week, as Griffin walked alone and un-aided from his workshop to the house on his parent's farm outside Mansfield, Texas, he began to see again for the first time in ten years.
Knowing that many cases of apparent blindness are relived by a shock, Griffin explained: "There was no bump. no jar. Nothing happened. Suddenly everything looked like red sand in front of my eyes." By the time a doctor arrived, Griffin could make out the color of his blue shirt and read a prescription blank. Near shock from the experience, Griffin was put on heavy doses of sedatives, given "cylinder glasses" to help pull his eye muscles back to useful strength. His vision, Griffin estimated, was about 20/150.

Although Griffin belittled the possibility, the only plausible medical explanation of his case was that his blindness had been mainly, if entirely hysterical, i.e, brought on by the emotional shock of bomb blasts. Dissolution of a long-standing blood clot could not explain his recovery, as such a clot would have soon caused irreparable damage to the eye's nerves. Seeing his wife and children for the first time, he said: "They are more beautiful than I ever suspected … I am astonished, stunned and grateful."

Doctors wanted him to go to a hospital where he could recuperate with proper rest and medication. Instead, he retreated to a sanctuary where he felt completely *cloistered*: a nearby Carmelite monastery.

Finally, the doctors decided to sequester me in a distant hospital. No more visitors, telephone calls or interviews. I requested that I be able to stay with the Carmelites instead of the hospital. The doctors thought that would even be better. So I was taken to Mount Carmel and no one knew I was being hidden. What the doctors did not know was that the monks would be tougher then they had been. The monks promised that I would be totally secluded and that the drugs would be administered strictly. I knew I would be safe in the cloister.

And he eventually answered a question many asked, who had heard of his remarkable transformation:

Many people wondered what it might be like to see again after a decade of blindness.

Sight does not return full-blown suddenly. You have to learn to see again, like a newborn infant. You have to learn to use muscles, to focus. The adjustment back to sight was as complex as the adjustment to blindness had been. The simple mechanics of living had to be learned over again. How to eat, how to walk, how to look at people. I kept forgetting that I could see, and that in seeing I could do many things I had put out of my life.

Griffin never really tried to ask the *how* of his recovery; the question of how it happened became supremely unimportant. The importance was that it *did* happen. (The probable cause was a severe concussion from the Japanese bombing and undetected diabetes.)

Just over two months later, Griffin was shaken by a household incident only he could fully appreciate:

March 12, 1957

I had an experience which I suppose only a few people in the world can understand. My heart is still pounding against my chest from it.

I went into my parents' house to get a cup of coffee. I decided to take the some pictures of the children since it was such a magnificent spring day. I went into the storeroom where I kept the camera and there, on a shelf, I saw my dark glasses which I wore when I was blind and my cane lying beside them. Both were covered with a thick layer of dust. It was so unexpected I was jarred. It was almost like walking upon a dead person. I slammed the door shut and returned to the living room.

"What's the matter?" my mother asked.

"Nothing," I said.

"Why, you're as pale as a ghost."

I could not tell her, but all of the horror of those past years exploded, smothering me. I went into mild shock, sweating, going white. I wanted desperately to take those glasses and throw them away with that film of dust on them. Strange, I saw nothing else in that cluttered store room.

I saw the cane too, but that did not matter. Only those terrible black glasses casting a dust-blurred highlight burned into my consciousness. They looked blind, staring.

Back in the world of sight, Griffin's first major writing job in the summer of 1958, was a "work for hire" project in Midland, Texas. He was approached by the First National Bank of Midland. To celebrate a new bank building, they wanted a special project—a history of the Midland area. Griffin was to be paid $10,000. to write the book. The book was to be given away by the bank—there was little distribution beyond the Midland area, surely no copies in bookstore across the country and no major sales to libraries.

But Griffin had led a hardscrabble life during the decade of his blindness. He took the bank's contract. And the book, *Land of the High Sky* illustrates how a talented writer can approach such a mundane project as the book for the bank. He first talked to two bank officials:

I asked Mr. Butler and Mr. Henderson to find me a place untouched, a place that would be as nearly as possible the way it had been when the first settler came to the Midland Country in 1882. I wanted to live alone with the type of equipment he might have carried. They contacted rancher Foy Proctor, who arranged to have me "deposited" on one of his ranches. They fixed me a bedroll, and I took along a coffee pot and some sandwiches. They left me at an isolated spot near a water hole where a stunted mesquite tree provided the only shade.

The immense silence emphasized my isolation. Grass-covered land stretched flat to all horizons. I left my bedroll at the pond and walked many miles that afternoon. The only sounds were my footsteps loud in the stillness and the occasional chirping of birds and a slight breeze in the brush. The sun baked down, but the breeze had a cool undercurrent.

When I retuned to the pond at sunset, I sat on my bedroll and began making notes. I built a small fire of dead mesquite branches and cooked coffee with water from the pond.

At dusk the jack rabbits came to the pond to drink. I looked up and saw them reflected in the still water. By 7:15, the sun had set. A luminous pink glow hung over the countryside and the breeze died to utter stillness. A full moon rose before the pink had faded.

Noiselessly a large sorrel horse appeared from the brush beyond the pool. He stared at me and after a long time he drank. Dampness and chill settled and the air grew fragrant with odors of sun-baked sands, animal scents and the smoke of my fire.

The horse left at a full run, a shadow dashing through the brush. I listened to his hooves rumbling the earth long after he disappeared.

I rolled out my bedroll, put my clothes under the canvas cover and slept in the chilling night. Throughout the night I made notes. One read:

11:30

I slept heavily and awakened. It is cold and still, though a faint breeze blows from the north. The moon is high now, but it does not obscure the stars. I added a log to the fire and it flames brightly again. Strange what a fire does. In this great deserted area, in these Carthusian silences, the circle of firelight dispells the forbidding aspects. However, the country, the plains stretch out beyond, and you cannot forget they are there. It is easy to erase the present, for nothing here is contemporary, nothing is changed from what it has always been. One feels joined to eternity, somehow. I begin to sense something of the hold this land has on people like J. Frank Dobie and Walter Prescott Webb—men who love its spaces, its silences.

I recall a letter from Dobie, in which he said: "Many times I feel more closely akin to the land and its native wild life than to people. Very few understand or care to understand the 'Bach Harmonies', the rhythms of the earth in its Wordsworthian 'diurnal round'."

Like the desert or the ocean, it throws a man face to face with nature stripped of all distracting elements—no mountains, no trees, no beautiful views, though its very simplicity is more than beauty. It overwhelms. To stay here, a man must face himself and the realities of life and death.

> I told myself this was the essence of it. Often
> I returned to the land and always its evocation
> grew more powerful. I could understand the
> early-day rancher's love for it and the cowboy's,
> as I could understand another's hatred of it.

Griffin's description of the vast plains reads very much like John Steinbeck's description of his native California in the pages of *Of Mice and Men*, published in 1937, especially in the early pages where Steinbeck describes the hobo campsites along the Salinas River.

Griffin began the chronicle of that land in 1849 and wrote of wagon trains, of Comanches, the *Llano Estacado* (the land of Staked Plains), how that area was impacted by the Civil War, the need for water, cattle drives, buffalo hunting, the advent of the railroads, drouths and blizzards, cowboys and the cowboy life, cattle and cattle ranching, and, of course, the rise of the banking business in the area. The growth of towns into cities, electricity, telephones, automobiles, discoveries of prehistoric life in the area, and much about the oil industry and the growth of Midland up to 1959.

At $10,000., the bank got its money's worth, but still he overcompensated. Returning to full eyesight and enthusiastic for even this "work for hire" project, Griffin's first draft exceeded 1,300 pages.

The final book, as printed, was 180 pages. And, for what it was, *Land of the High Sky* is still readable as a history of that area of Texas.

Five |

The Second of Three

Sprigle, Griffin, Halsell...

THOSE WHO KNOW of John Howard Griffin's odyssey into the vicious heart of the south, may assume it was the only journey of its kind ever taken, but in fact, Griffin's remarkably brave moral decision and dangerous odyssey was the second of three of its kind: the first has largely been forgotten.

Ray Sprigle's name was not exactly unknown in the newspaper world before his trip into the land of Jim Crow. His stories of Supreme Court Hugo Black's connection with the Ku Klux Klan won him the Pulitzer Prize in 1938, and in 1944 the Headliners' Club presented him a medal for his series about the black market in meat. He dug out the information for the series by posing as a black-market butcher. Similarly, he took a job as an attendant in several state institutions, while gathering material for a series on Pennsylvania's mental hospitals in 1947 and worked as a coal miner for another story.

Sprigle attended Ohio State University for one year and left. He took a job with the now long-defunct *Ohio Sun* in Columbus, then, as was then the custom, became something of a newspaper vagabond, working on ten different midwestern newspapers, some for only a few days, some for as much as a year. He did take a longer job at the *Pittsburgh Post*, working his way up to city editor, but preferred writing and so returned to that.

Sprigle wrote a series of articles for *The Pittsburgh Post-Gazette* in 1948, which were turned into a 30-chapter book, *In the Land of Jim Crow*, released first as a pamphlet form as *I Was a Negro in the South for Thirty Days* and subsequently published in book form by Simon and Schuster in 1949.

> ... in more than six months of searching, I couldn't discover any lotion, liquid, unguent or chemical that would turn a white hide brown or black and remain impervious to perspiration, soap and water, and the ravages of the ordinary wear and tear of daily life.
> ... I tried iodine, argyrol, pryogallic acid, potassium permanganate. Come a little perspiration and I'd find myself striped like a tiger or spotted like a leopard.

He finally got a three-week suntan in Florida; his disguise for traveling throughout the south as a black man for four weeks was then simplicity itself. If asked, he simply *said* he was a black man, leaving the questioner to assume he was a very light-light-light-skinned black man.

He buttressed that, if needed, with a paper trail of documents:

> I became James Rayel Crawford, Negro, from Pittsburgh, come south to visit friends. I built up an identity as a not too industrious small-time writer and small-time office holder and had the necessary papers to prove it. I never got a chance to show them to anyone. Without question, I became "Brother Crawford," welcomed wherever we went with generous hospitality and heart-warming friendliness.

He apparently never need to use the documents he had prepared to prove he was James Rayel Crawford. In the Foreword, Margaret Halsey wrote:

> Mr. Sprigle's report on what it feels like to live as a second-class citizen reads, to the first-class citizen, like sociological Jules Verne. There are so many things one hadn't thought of! What do you do if your wife needs a Caesarian section and no hospital within eighty miles will admit her because she is colored? If you are a Negro parent, at what age do you explain to your wide-eyed children that they must adjust to a life of permanent humiliation?
>
> Mr. Sprigle has not turned up any new material. All his facts have been reported before in such research volumes as Gunnar Myrdal's *An American Dilemma*, and others. But in the scholarly disquisitions, the facts are necessarily arranged in graphs and statistics and

cautious footnotes. In Mr. Sprigle's book they are personal and vivid—the spontaneous, unstudied reactions of a self- respecting white American trying to live from one dawn to the next under the disabilities imposed on colored Americans.

That Mr. Sprigle is courageous, his assignments attests. But in the view of the importance and intricacy of the whole subject. It is only fair to ask whether he is also impartial and objective. To which the answer is, he was impartial and objective when he started, and when he was finished he was still objective.

Finally, she wrote:

There are only two possible solutions to the problem of human relationships between white and non-white Americans. One is the ethical solution and the other is the unethical solution. It is too soon to be comfortably sure, as yet, in which direction the country will move, but there have been signs of late that the forces of progress are pulling slightly ahead. If they are, some credit is certainly due to those American journalists who apply their techniques directly and without evasion to the American scene.

Sprigle's *In the Land of Jim Crow* contains chapters on ...

... sharecropping ...

You begin to get a better idea of what it means to be a black sharecropper in the South as you sit on a homemade stool in the two-room shack of Henry Williams in Sumter County on the road to Americus in the Georgia cotton country. No Northern farmer would keep his cattle in a shanty like this. And this place of Henry's is far better than hundreds of others we have passed on the roads.

At least it has one window in one room. Many of these sharecropper cabins have none at all—just holes in the wall with a wooden shutter that can be closed against the sleet and the cold of the winter. And when you close the shutter you shut out the light too, so you live for five months of the year in a dismal black cavern. In the summer you can leave your shutters open to the sunlight and wind—and also to the flies, mosquitoes and sundry other insects.

Henry, however, has no fault to find with his mansion. "Yessir," he says, "got us four rooms here." The two-room discrepancy between Henry's account and mine is due to a rough board lean-to slapped against the back of his shack and is bisected by a board partition. In one half of the the place is a rather hopeless stove where Mrs. Williams does her cooking. At that, she's far better off than scores of her neighbors up and down the road. They do their cooking in an open fireplace—with a kettle for collards or turnip greens, a skillet for fat-back, and the corn pone basked in ashes.

Henry has been a sharecropper for twenty-nine years, he tells me.

"You been making any money these few years back with cotton and peanuts bring big prices?" I ask him.

"You don't make any money sharecroppin'," he replies, surprised at the question. "Some years you get some cash in the fall. Bad years you jest go over to the next year."

... violence ...

She is worn and aged and bent beyond her time. Her hands are warped and gnarled as she wrings them helplessly. Nearly a quarter of a century behind a plow and mule under blazing Georgia suns have done that to her.

In a haze of dull despair, this broken, hopeless Negro farm woman sits in the drab, neat little parlor in black Atlanta an tells her tale of wanton murder. Terror and tragedy seemingly have wrung her dry of emotion.

"When the white folks gave him back to me he was in his coffin. I held his hands when I kissed him. And I felt the broken pieces of bone under the skin. It was just like a sackful of little pieces of bone.

"I put my hands around him for one last time as he lay there. All down one side of him there were no ribs—just pieces that moved when I held him.'

That was her husband she was talking about—Henry Gilbert, forty-two years old, Negro farmer, murdered by the white folks of Harris and Troup Counties, Georgia, May 29, 1947.

... and separate but equal ...

So this is what "separate but equal" means!

Right here, within the space of little more than a thousand yards along the highway, that hard-worked phrase—beloved catchword of every Southern apologist for discrimination against little black children—becomes an evil, despicable mockery.

This thing is a school, this dilapidated, sagging old shack, leaning and lopsided as its makeshift foundations crumble. It is the kind of school that the white folks of Clay County provide for Negro children, here on the outskirts of the pleasant, thriving little Georgia town of Bluffton.

Well, surely this ancient tumble-down pile of lumber is "separate" enough.

But as far as the "equal" of the phrase goes—to just what is this old hovel equal?

Certainly not to the attractive, modern school plant just a little was down the road toward Bluffton. That fine brick structure is the kind of school that Clay County white folks build and maintain for their own children.

The contrast is deadly. But here on the short stretch of Georgia highway is the completely accurate picture of the South's Jim Crow educational system.

All this was written five years before the segregationist Jim Crow laws were broken with the Supreme Court decision Brown v. Board of Education, in 1954. The Jim Crow laws had been the laws of the land ever since Plessy v. Ferguson in 1896, which legitimized "separate but equal," 58 years previously.

In the Land of Jim Crow and *Black like Me* are hauntingly similar, with some stylistic differences.

Both were first published as a series of articles; Sprigle's in *The Pittsburgh Post-Gazette* and Griffin's in

Sepia magazine, as a series "Journey into Shame," and the travel involved was financed by both publications.

Chapter titles for *Inside the Land of Jim Crow* read like newspaper headlines:

Into a Black World
Not Quite Slavery—Not Quite Freedom
The Problem of "Passing"
Southern Hospitality—Negro Style
Don't "Figure Behind the Man"
Negroes Too, are Different
"Justifiable Homicide in Self-Defense"

... and other similar chapter titles.

Black Like Me is written in a diary form and the chapter titles reinforce that timeline:

October 28, 1959
October 29
October 30
November 1
November 2
November 6
November 7

... and on, throughout the text.

Both are, of necessity, written in the first-person narrative form. Sprigle's book begins:

I was a Negro in the Deep South.
Now, I, a "white" man, know, as well as any
white man may, what it means to be a black man

below the Mason and Dixon line—the Smith and Wesson line to us black folk.

For four endless, fear-filled weeks, along with the ten million other Negroes of the South, I lived under the burden of the Jim Crow system, with its iniquitous pattern of oppression and cruelty and discrimination.

I ate, slept, traveled, lived black. I lodged in Negro households. I ate in Negro restaurants. I crept through the back and side doors of railroad and bus stations. I traveled Jim Crow in trains and busses and streetcars and taxicabs.

It was a strange, new—and for me, uncharted—world that I entered when, in a Jim Crow railroad coach, we rumbled across the Potomac out of Washington. It was a world of which I had no remote conception, despite scores of trips throughout the south. The world I had known in the south was white. Now I was black and the world I was to know was as bewildering as if I had been dropped down on the moon.

Griffin's book begins:

For years the idea had haunted me, and that night it returned more insistently than ever.

If a white man became a Negro in the Deep South, what adjustments would he have to make? What is it like to experience discrimination based on skin color, something over which one had no control?

This speculation was sparked again by a report that lay on my desk in the old barn that served as my office. The report mentioned the rise in suicide tendency among Southern Negroes. This did not mean that they killed themselves, but rather that they had reached a stage where they simply no longer cared whether they lived or died.

And, he wrote ...

How else except by becoming a Negro could a white man hope to learn the truth? Though we lived side by side throughout the South, communication between the two races had simply ceased to exist. Neither really knew what went on with those of the other race. The Southern Negro will not tell the white man the truth. He long ago learned that if he speaks a truth unpleasing to the white, the white will make life miserable.

The only way I could see to bridge the gap between us was to become a Negro. Now I decided I would do this.

Both Sprigle and Griffin shaved their heads prior to beginning their odysseys throughout the south.

Both had congenial traveling companions; Sprigle for his complete trip, Griffin for part of his.

Sprigle took the train south from Washington D.C., and rode with Walter White, executive director of the National Association for the Advancement of Colored People. White traveled with Sprigle throughout the four-week trek through the south. White was the ideal choice for the journey. Sprigle remembered clearly White's companionship:

We'd roll along through the night, our destination the Negro section of a town perhaps two hundred miles a way and for hours, I'd listen while he recited long passages from *Macbeth* and *Hamlet*, Ingersoll's essay on Napoleon—page after page from the best in English literature. All his life he has fought against the oppression, the injustice and the discrimination weighing on his people. But there is no bitterness, no hatred in the man. To him, his "Southland," as he always calls it, is the fairest country in the land. He loves his Georgia above all states—he would live nowhere else in America.

Griffin shared a bus ride with a man he described as "a striking Negro man, tall slender, elegently-dressed—the 'Valentino' type. He wore a mustache and neatly trimmed beard" and, Griffin, observed, he "spoke fragments of French, Spanish and Japanese."

The man's name was Christophe.

He punched his hat back, concentrated, stiffened his hand, palms upward, in a supplicating gesture and began softly to chant *Tantum ergo sacramentum, Veneremur cernui* in as beautiful Latin as I have ever heard. I stared at him dumbfounded as he chanted the Gregorian version of this famous text.

He made a huge sign of the cross, lowered his head and recited, again with perfect Latin diction, the *Confiteor*. When it was over, he remained still, in profound introspection. Above the hum of the bus's wheels on the pavement, silence surrounded us. No one spoke. Doubtless those nearest us who had witnessed the strange scene were perplexed.

"You were an altar boy, I guess," I said.

"I was," he said, not raising his head. "I wanted to be a priest."

For self-protection, both Sprigle and Griffin became quietly passive, deferential toward whites, and non-commnicative except when necessary.

And the moral outrage they felt is identical on each page of both books.

The only difference of any consequence was that of Sprigle's constant companion, Walter White; Griffin never had the companionship of anyone traveling with him and no safety net of any sort. Griffin simply did not want to expose anyone else to the dangers of his journey.

Griffin never knew about Sprigle's *In the Land of Jim Crow*; it was published while Griffin was blind, and during that decade, he read (or had read to him) no American writing. He spent most of those years listening to tapes provided by philosopher Jacques Maritain and Father Stanley Murphy of Canada, founder of The Christian Culture series.

The final third book in this unofficial trilogy was Grace Halsell's *Soul Sister*, published in 1969, eight years after *Black Like Me*.

Halsell was a free-lance journalist working as a Presidential aide in the White House in the Lyndon Johnson administration, and was attending a State Department reception, when an acquaintance mentioned *Black Like Me*:

> The title meant nothing to me. Perhaps I was in Turkey, Korea or Arabia when the book came out. And I hadn't heard of the author, John Howard Griffin, although we came from the same town, Fort Worth, Texas. The next

day I bought *Black Like Me* and plunged into
it, discovering Griffin talked to me like an inner voice, calm, suggestive. "I could do that ... I
could be black."

Even thinking about being black caused the
same confusing doppelgänger *Other* effect Griffin
experienced:

> The seed is planted, it grows. I have not
> reasoned it there nor nourished it logically.
> Imagination, feeling, cause it to grow. (And
> what makes men different could be feeling
> rather than reason.) I had only to imagine my-
> self black and them, for the first time, I saw my-
> self *white*! This puzzled me, unsettled me.

Halsell arranged to meet Griffin in Baltimore, where
he was giving a speech. She suggested they drive to
Washington, D.C., getting acquainted along the way and
Griffin could take a plane from Washington to his next
stop.

They ate dinner in her apartment and she finally
gave him a memo, detailing what she wanted to do.

> He read it quietly, and with great feeling re-
> sponded immediately: "*Oh yes, you have to do it.*"
> Griffin said he had always wished a woman
> could do what he had done, because there were
> so many feelings that black women must have—
> watching their beloved children grow up to be
> despised by some simply because of the color of
> their skin—and that he could never penetrate
> the feelings of a woman, of a mother as I might
> be able to do. He said that since he had written
> *Black Like Me* many women had come to him

with the idea that they might try what he did. "But I discouraged every one, because—until you—I never met anyone I thought could do it."

The next day—April 4, 1968, Halsell was on Lyndon Johnson's presidential plane, Air Force One enroute from Washington, D.C, to Texas, when she learned Martin Luther king Jr. had been shot. *One can kill a person, but not a dream,* she remembered thinking.

She visited Griffin at his home and met his family—the visit only buoyed her dream.

She returned to Washington and visited a doctor, Robert Stolar. He needed only to write her a prescription.

> After I take the medication? "You will be very black ..." Dr. Stolar said. "You might stay dark for a year."

She got contact lenses. Black ones. Her blue eyes could have revealed her secret.

She asked Aaron Lerner, a doctor at the Yale Medical Center specifically about drugs:

> What about the medication psoralen, I wanted to know.
>
> He told me the medical term was trimethyl psoralen, and said the label generally used is "trisoralen." Originally, he said, the medicine came from a plant in Egypt, but when it became difficult to secure, it was produced synthetically.
>
> He explained that skin color comes principally from the dark pigment melanin (produced in cells known as melanocytes, sandwiched

between outer and inner skin layers). The quality and distribution of melanin causes skin to be different colors in different parts of the body, and also plays the major role in the gradation of colors that is found from one individual to another.

The drug psoralen, taken orally before exposure to sunlight or ultraviolet light, steps up the melanin-production process and turns light skin dark.

Lerner repeated what she had heard before: "In two or three weeks you will be *very dark*." She also got a walnut stain, actually potassium permanganate, as a supplement.

Slowly, slowly, she changed. She became "high yellar."

> At the bank, a woman teller: "Oh, what a tan." (Pause) "it looks so—*deep*."
> At the health club: "My you have a good tan." (Pause) "You are almost *black!*"

She flew to Puerto Rico to complete her transformation.

Then Grace Halsell went to New York City.

> Yes, I've packed all of my own fears, right in with the nylons and hairbrush. I'm not supposed to go there.... The white man says the black man is a beast and marauder, he will rape you, rob you, he is man as the devil (you know the devil has to be black). This mythology makes me a trespasser: I go where I have no "right" to be; my world won't condone it; my people won't understand.

Halsell moves to Harlem, and, like Griffin, becomes lost as an *Other* ...

> I keep walking, clinging to the thought
> that there's always room for one more, always
> a room at the inn, just the right place is going
> to turn up. I pass the Black Panther headquar-
> ters, in an area where Harlem again presents
> a scene of despair and debasement: liquor s
> stores, bars, beauty shops, small stores, small
> cares—no business you'd term "black business."
> And the people walking a round imprisoned in
> an open-air jail, as if the place doesn't belong to
> them and they too, are transient here.

> It's not that the people are starving to death
> (my mind conjures up the thin sticks of bones
> strewn like debris, those dead and dying of
> India). And the people are not even *dirt* poor,
> like the poor of Paraguay, who live on the dirt
> and can extract edible roots from it. No, it is
> rather that here in Harlem they are reminded
> that they are the poorest of the poor in an afflu-
> ent society because they have been denied their
> *dreams* and the American promise is a worth-
> less lie.

Griffin saw the world in part, with medicine and mu-sic; Halsell saw it in terms of artists, when she visited a Harlem hospital:

> I study the faces and am startled by the
> agony and grief etched on them. This is pre-
> cisely the way Goya and Daumier had painted
> the poor, the destitute, the forgotten people

who have suffered beyond human capacity to endure, but somehow have gone on enduring as "faceless" women and men.

Taking a taxi into Harlem once, Halsell fails to tip the driver and hears the same profanities that Griffin heard on the New Orleans bus:

> "Hey! Stupid! What y'gonna give me for driving you here?" he yells. As I struggle to move my gear to the sidewalk, he continues his tirade. "Ask me to drive you to this hell-hole, don't give me nuthin'—you stupid black *bitch*!"

Grace Halsell had ventured into Harlem alone. "Harlem in some ways is like a cemetery," she wrote, "those who are 'in' don't feel they can get out and those who are 'out' don't want to get in."

She journeyed to the south and discovered years after the Jim Crow laws were broken, old codes remained the same. She boarded a bus in New Orleans headed for Mississippi:

> With three or four exceptions, those aboard the bus are all black. When the bus rolls into a terminal only those who have reached their destination are permitted to disembark. In this way the blacks don't really integrate the terminals by using the restrooms or restaurants. We are like prisoners, never being able to get off during a long journey to stretch our legs, buy a newspaper, or cup of coffee. The basic needs of nature must be met in a small toilet in the back of the bus.

Conditions Halsell encountered in the south in 1969 seemed largely unchanged from those Ray Sprigle observed during the Jim Crow years of 1949. And before her journey into Harlem and then into the south, she told a black lawyer in Washington, D.C. she had planned to become black and eventually go into the south.

"You will go there and *get yourself killed*," he said.

Ray Sprigle may have anticipated that; John Howard Griffin certainly did.

Six |

The South

"Now you go into oblivion ..."

October, 1959
Mansfield, Texas

WHY DID GRIFFIN take the dangerous and yet courageous step of dying his skin black to make the journey
throughout the south to eventually write *Black Like
Me*? He could have answered this in any number of
ways, but the most succinct is told in Robert Bonazzi's
Man in the Mirror:

> "The real story is the universal one of men
> who destroy the souls and bodies of other men
> (and in the process destroy themselves) for rea-
> sons neither really understands. It is the story
> of the persecuted, the defrauded, the feared
> and detested." This universal story of persecu-
> tion—man's inhumanity to man—has been told
> in countless variations by every culture in all
> historical epochs—right up to the preset.

"I could have been a Jew in Germany, a
Mexican in a number of states of a member of
any 'inferior' group," he insisted. "Only the de-
tails would have differed. The story would be
the same. *Black Like Me* is, of course, the historical record of what it was like to be a Negro
in the Deep South prior to the civil-rights era
of the 1960s. It is also an intensively lived experience, evoked by the immediacy of his vital,
vivid prose, that has kept open a window on
that historical time and place.

Why he did it, he later said, was a question that
black people *never* asked him.

He also had to face the question of the *Other*. Griffin
was always, by instinct, a cultural anthropologist, or
ethnologist, and he encountered a wide variety of situations that raised the question, as he phrased it, of the
Other. The outsider in a strange culture; oppressed minorities in a variety of cultures; the outsider unable to
communicate; the sense of modern humanity lost in
the world.

He had seen it as a young American in French
schools (a benign version of *Other*-ness, easily con-
quered in large part by learning French); he had seen
in during his stays in the monasteries in France, when
he was the outsider in the close-knit priesthood of the
Benedictine orders; he had seen it when the Nazis
came for Jews and other non-Aryans; he had seen it
in the desert island in the South Pacific when he was
the *other*, led through the jungle by a five-year old boy,
unable to cope in a primitive world, as a twentieth century urban male. And he had surely became the *other*,

during his decade of blindness when he was trapped in a sightless world, an outcast, with his black glasses and white cane, stigmatized as helpless by the sighted world.

Now he would be the *Other* in the south, a stranger in a strange land.

Griffin began his odyssey October 28, 1959 considering the proposal, which was "suddenly mysterious and frightening." The next day he drove to Fort Worth and talked to George Levitan, publisher of *Sepia*, a general circulation magazine for blacks, that was designed like *Life* or *Look*. Griffin explained his proposal to Levitan, who was both surprised and skeptical. His reaction and the reaction of other staff members of *Sepia* was: *you don't know what you're getting into.* But Levitan agreed to underwrite Griffin's expenses and Griffin agreed to contribute articles about his experiences to *Sepia*. Griffin also met with FBI officials in Dallas; their reaction was: it was out of our jurisdiction, they said and, oh yes, you don't know what you're getting into.

Griffin told his wife, what he was planning. After recovering from her astonishment, she said, *if that's what you have to do, that's what you have to do.* Griffin never offered to take her along. It would altogether be too dangerous; dangerous enough for himself, impossibly dangerous to take his wife along.

Griffin traveled to New Orleans November 1. He had a sumptuous meal at Broussard's, in the French Quarter, then the next day, called three dermatologists and made an appointment with the first one.

A common question, throughout the years always has been: how did he change his skin? The dermatologist used a treatment for vitiligo, a skin condition in which white spots appear on the face and body. The chemical was Oxsoralen and the treatment should have taken six weeks to eight months to darken the skin, but Griffin decided he could not wait that long and began accelerated treatments.

His treatment regimen was dangerous. He had to be closely monitored and checked for liver damage. The dermatologist gave him a prescription for Oxsoralen and recommended lengthy sunlamp treatments. He spent up to 15 hours a day for a week under a sunlamp, wearing cotton pads to protect his eyes. The only side effects were fatigue and nausea.

Griffin spent some of this time as a guest of Harold and Gladys Levy, who had previously introduced him to Sadie Jacobs; she, in turn, had taught him how to use a flexible white cane, and how to navigate the streets of New Orleans, while he was blind.

He didn't live in the Levy's home, but rather a guest house, which had been a former slave quarters. Becoming a black man while living in a slave cabin was an irony not lost on Griffin. He did not mention them by name in *Black Like Me*, to protect them for any possible consequences.

The last appointment with the dermatologist was November 7, 1959.

The dermatologist established the daily dosage of Oxsoralen and informed Griffin that if the dosage was discontinued, his skin would slowly lighten. If the dosage was begun again, his skin would slowly darken again.

He showed, as Griffin recalled, "much doubt and perhaps regret that he had ever cooperated with me in this transformation."

The doctor shook Griffin's hand solemnly and then said, "now you go into oblivion."

The doctor suggested that Griffin shave his head; he simply didn't show the characteristics of being black, with his natural hair.

Alone, near dark, Griffin began to shave his head by feel; he had learned how to shave while blind, so shaving his head offered no problem, although it was tedious. He applied coat after coat of stain, washing away the excess. He showered, washing away more excess stain. Only then, did he venture a look at what he had become:

> Turning off all the lights, I went into the bathroom and closed the door. I stood in the darkness before the mirror, my hand on the light switch. I forced myself to flick it on.
>
> In the flood of light against white tile, the face and shoulders of a stranger—a fierce, bald, very dark Negro—glared at me from the glass. He in no way resembled me.
>
> The transformation was total and shocking. I had expected to see myself disguised, but this was something else. I was imprisoned in the flesh of an utter stranger, an unsympathetic one with whom I felt no kinship. All traces of John Howard Griffin I had been were wiped from existence. Even the senses underwent a change so profound it filled me with distress. I looked into a mirror and saw nothing of the white John Howard Griffin's past. No, the reflections

led back to Africa, back to the shanty and the ghetto, back to the fruitless struggles against the mark of blackness. Suddenly, almost with no mental preparation, no advance hint, it became clear and permeated my whole being. My inclination was to fight against it. I had gone too far. I knew now there is no such thing as a disguised white man, when the black won't rub off. The black man is wholly a Negro, regardless of what he once may have been. I was a newly created Negro who must go out that door and live in a world unfamiliar to me.

The completeness of this transformation appalled me. It was unlike anything I had ever imagined. I became two men, the observing one and the one who panicked, who felt Negroid even into the depths of his entrails. I felt the beginnings of great loneliness, not because I was a Negro, but because the man I had been, the self I knew, was hidden in the flesh of another. If I returned home to my wife and children they would not know me. They would open the door and stare blankly at me. My children would want to know who is this large, bald Negro. If I walked up to friends, I knew I would see no flicker of recognition in their eyes.

I had tampered with the mystery of existence and I had lost the sense of my own being. That is what devastated me. The Griffin that was had become invisible.

The word in German is *doppelgänger*: the ghostly counterpart of a living person, but *doppelgänger* makes no reference to this sort of second self.

In *Man in the Mirror*, Robert Bonazzi writes:

This seminal passage from *Black Like Me* reads like a "shock of recognition" scene in a modern literary novel. But there is a curious inversion for, in fact, the passage is most notable for its lack of recognition. Within that illuminated exposure, Griffin's entire psyche was overwhelmed by a series of nearly simultaneous disruptions. His involuntary reaction to that sudden crisis was massive denial.

On the sensory plane, he seemed to conjure a visual distortion. What his eyes saw, his mind refused to perceive. The dualistic subject-object relation was short-circuited by the unexpected "stranger" glaring back from the glass. But who glared at whom? Was Griffin that dark reflection in the mirror or was he the inner white consciousness that reflected upon it?

This disembodied image stunned his ego into temporary dysfunction. Coherence disintegrated, continuity ceased, identity disappeared. The transformation obscured the outward appearance by which he could be recognized by those who knew him, severing him from all that had been familiar. even his own name—recalled three times as if to declare individuality—echoed like a litany of disconnection and loss.

Unconsciously, Griffin had projected a primordial shadow figure, causing him to recoil from the truth. The repressed prejudices he had managed for so long to deny or rationalize were exposed with brutal clarity in the "stranger's" glare. The shadow figure was none other than the *Other*—the beast from the jungle of his deepest shame. Without warning, Griffin encountered his own racism face to face.

Seven |

The *Other*

... through a crude but mysterious alchemy ...

November 7, 1959
New Orleans

IN BLACK LIKE ME, Griffin implies he was in a hotel
when the transformation was made; in fact he was in the
slave cabin owned by his friends the Levys. After shaving and staining his head dark by feel, he had turned off
all the lights in the room, went to the bathroom, waited
for his eyes to adjust to the dark, then turned on the
light and saw himself in the mirror. It was midnight.

He remembers thinking:

"I was a man born old at midnight into a
new life. How does such a man act?"

Griffin clearly did not comprehend the moral complexities of what he had done; he continued to wrestle

with a myriad of implications of his journey into the
Other.

Biographer Robert Bonazzi wrote:

> Through a crude but mysterious alchemy,
> his scientific experiment had been transformed
> into a life-study; the seclusion of midnight had
> changed into a secret human laboratory. Since
> it was "a new life" into which even this "man
> born old" entered, the inevitable results would
> be fresh and fascinating, because the manchild
> became both the experimentor and the body of
> experimentation.

Griffin took a bus and although the New Orleans
transit system was no longer segregated, he took a seat
at the back of the bus. He found the Butler hotel and sat
down in the restaurant. A large black man observed his
bald head and was instantly amused—baldness means
virility.

> Within less than two hours, Griffin had
> traveled a long psychic road, from feeling that
> his white identity has been usurped by a black
> man to being that bald black man in the eyes of
> all he encountered—black and white—including
> the fellow who called him Slick because bald-
> ness was a new emblem of virility!

In a subsequent essay, "The Intrinsic *Other*,"
he explained how he continued to wrestle with the
implications:

> Almost the deepest shock I had came the
> first night I went out into the New Orleans

night as a Negro. I went to a hotel in the ghetto
and took the best available room—a tawdry,
miserable little cubbyhole. I sat on the bed and
glanced at myself in the mirror on the wall. For
the first time I was alone as a Negro in the community. That glance brought a sickening shock
that I tried not to admit, not to recognize, but I
could not avoid it. It was the shock of seeing my
face in the mirror and of feeling an involuntary
movement of antipathy for that face, because it
was pigmented, the face of a Negro.

I realized then that although intellectually I
had liberated myself from the prejudices which
our Southern tradition inculcates in us, these
prejudices were so indredged in me that at the
emotional level I was in no way liberated. I was
filled with despair.

He saw all this as an epiphany....

(He had) come all this way, had myself
transformed chemically into a black man, *because of* my profound intellectual convictions
about racism, only to find that my own prejudices, at the emotional level, were hopelessly
ingrained in me.

His first few hours had become an almost horrific
version of the German idea of the *doppelgänger*—the
ghostly second self.

Griffin's learning experiences continued. He took a
bus and sat halfway from the front; not deliberately in
the back. When the bus became crowded and a white
woman entered, he rose to give her his seat, then

suddenly realized that wasn't done—*to give up your seat would be to lose.* Other Negroes stared at him with disapproval. He tried to make eye contact with the white woman.

Her face hardened. "What are you looking at me like *that* for?"

The simple act of attempting to give up his seat became an example of the universal stereotype of a black man lusting after a white woman. He then sat "sphinxlike," understanding that the Negroes on the bus resented him for the attention he caused.

Then he heard it:

> I learned a strange thing—that in a jumble
> of unintelligent talk, the word "nigger" leaps
> out with electric clarity. You always hear it and
> it always stings.

It had been aimed at him.

The next morning Griffin began the arduous task of being black. Before his transformation in the Levy's slave cabin, Griffin had gotten his shoes shined, at a French quarter shoeshine stand. He returned, for another shoeshine—and more. Griffin seemed to enjoy the moment:

> "Is there something familiar about these
> shoes?
> "Yeah—I been shining some for a white man ..."
> "A fellow named Griffin?"
> "Yeah," he straightened up, "Do you know him?"
> "I am him."

The shoeshine man, Sterling Williams, was dumb-founded. But Griffin reminded him of the previous conversations they had and Williams became convinced Griffin had been the white man of the previous days.

Williams not only became Griffin's mentor, but a co-conspirator.

It was not the first time in Griffin's life that he had adopted a mentor.

> Because Williams had mastered the survival techniques that worked in that segregated system, Griffin was raptly attentive to the elder black man's wisdom. Choosing Williams to be his mentor was a new variation on Griffin's old pattern of becoming a student under an accomplished guide. In the past he had chosen experts in the fields of his pursuit, mentors who were the embodiment of the ideals he cherished.

... Griffin biographer Robert Bonazzi wrote. And Griffin later said:

> Most of these people taught me, or showed me, by example ... the real meaning of labor, or the total gift of self, as the only possible way to fruition in any field.... I learned the value of total isolation in work, of following one's own path, of remaining close to the soul's recognition of reality, of taking the chance.

Williams began to teach Griffin, in hushed tones and sideways glances to make sure no one was overhearing them, how to behave. Their conversations, if overheard, would have seemed ludicrous to any bystander: one black man instructing another black man, furtively and in conspiratorial tones, how to be black. Williams relished the role.

Griffin asked if he could stay and shine shoes for a while. Williams agreed, but said Griffin was "'way too well dressed for a shine boy." Griffin shined shoes then too, and gave the proceeds to Williams. Their conversations became completely conspiratorial; Williams began to use the "we" form and discussed "our situation":

> The illusion of my "Negro-ness" took over so completely that I fell into the same pattern of talking and thinking. It was my first intimate glimpse. We were Negroes and our concern was the white man and how to get along with him; how to hold our own and raise ourselves in his esteem without for one moment letting him think he had any God-given rights that we did not also have.

Griffin learned other lessons at the shine stand. White men would approach, get a shine, be 'way more than friendly and then ask where they could find a Negro girl. Williams had learned long previously, how to spot those men; Griffin soon learned too. "When they want to sin, they're very democratic," Williams said.

A black woman in a white dress approached the shine stand and spoke briefly with Williams, then with Griffin. He was perplexed by the encounter. She was, Williams said after she left, a widow looking for a mate. She had apparently chosen Griffin. He had to try and think of a discreet way out of that possible predicament. He subsequently told her he was married, but she was not wholly deterred.

The survival techniques learned at the shoeshine stand allowed Griffin to fully enter his new world.

Griffin found the YMCA Coffee Shop, and with the help of YMCA clerks, rented a room next door. He returned to the YMCA and met Reverend A.L Davis, a Mr. Gayle, a civic leader and bookstore owner, and others, and, Griffin observed "my feeling of disorientation diminished for a time."

And yet ... and yet....

Griffin walked through New Orleans ...

> On Chartres Street in the French Quarter, I walked toward Brennan's one of New Orleans' famous restaurants. Forgetting myself for a moment, I stopped to study the menu that was elegantly exposed in a show window. I read, realizing that a few days earlier I could have gone in and ordered anything on the menu. But now, though I was the same person with the same appetite, the same appreciation and even the same wallet, no power on earth could get me inside this place for a meal. I kept hearing some Negro say, "You can live here all your life, but you'll never get inside one of the great restaurants except as a kitchen boy." The Negro often dreams of things separated from him only by a door, knowing that he is forever cut off from experiencing them.

And yet ... and yet....

As Griffin walked through the streets of New Orleans he was once taunted by a white bully. Time and again. "Hey Mr. No-Hair ... Hey Mr. Baldy ... Shithead...."

Griffin finally stepped into an alley and bluffed him: "You follow me, boy, 'cause I'm just aching to feed you a fistful of brass knucks right in that big mouth of yours ..." Griffin prayed and prayed. "Blessed St. Jude, send the bastard away." When he looked the bully was gone.

He hurried to the nearby St. John the Baptist Catholic Church. As he sat on the outside steps, the church bell chimed eight. Griffin heard other sounds:

> The word "nigger" picked up the bell's reso-
> nances and repeated itself again and again in
> my brain.
> *Hey nigger, you can't go in there.*
> *Hey nigger, you can't drink here.*
> *We don't serve niggers.*
> And the white bully's taunts: *Mr. No-Hair,*
> *Mr. Baldy, Shithead....*
> And the last words from the dermatologist:
> *Now you go into oblivion.*

Griffin felt buoyed by his cordial conversations in the New Orleans YMCA, but that euphoria did not last. He planned to take a bus heading into Mississippi. He suspected Mississippi would be worse than New Orleans. He was right. But he didn't even get into Mississippi before his euphoria disappeared. He went to the bus station to ask about a bus to Hattiesburg. The clerk ...

> answered rudely and glared at me with
> such loathing I knew I was receiving what the
> Negroes call "the hate stare." It was my first
> experience with it. This was so exaggeratedly
> hateful I could have been amused if I had not
> been so surprised.

Griffin sat waiting for the bus.

Once again a "hate stare" drew my attention like a magnet. It came from a middle-aged, heavyset, well-dressed white man. He sat a few yards away, fixing his eyes on me. Nothing can describe the withering horror of this. You feel lost, sick at heart before such unmasked hatred, not so much because it threatens you as because it shows humans in such an inhuman light. You see a kind of insanity, something so obscene the very obscenity of it (rather than its threat) terrifies you. It was so new I could not take my eyes from the man's face. I felt like saying: "What in God's name are you doing to yourself?"

Earlier he had bought an assortment of books at a Catholic book store, titles by St. Thomas Aquinas, Jacques Maritain and others. While waiting for the bus, he picked one up at random. The pages fell open and he read:

> ... it is by justice that we can authentically measure man's value or his nullity ... the absence of justice is the absence of what makes him a man. —Plato.

Griffin remembered reading the same dictum another way:

> He who is less than just is less than man.

On the bus Griffin meets Christophe, one of the more memorable figures in *Black Like Me*, a comic yet tragic figure. On the bus ride through Mississippi, the driver stopped for a ten-minute restroom stop. He allowed the whites to get off, but barred Griffin and other Negroes from leaving the bus. Earlier, on a New Orleans city bus, the driver deliberately drove eight blocks past where Griffin wanted off, before stopping. Griffin had to walk the eight blocks back. These incidents were, Griffin rue-fully understood, racial cat-and-mouse games played all too often in New Orleans, as well as places like Mississippi.

On the bus, Griffin is given the name and address of a safe contact in Hattiesburg; the first address led him to a second contact point, then to a third. As he was walking down a dark, deserted street, a car full of white boys yelled obscenities at him and threw some-time at him, an orange or a tangerine, perhaps. He be-came overwhelmed by a sense of panic—and terror. The third contact point was an upper room in a shanty that seemed to have never been painted.

Griffin became overcome by the sense of the *Other*— and he may very well have vividly remembered hiding from the Gestapo in France before fleeing to England. Just as before, when he had first seen the *Other*, by looking into a mirror in the Levy's slave cabin, Griffin again looked into a mirror ...

> I switched on the light and looked into a cracked piece of mirror bradded with bent nails to the wall. The bald Negro stared back at me from its mottled sheen. I knew I was in hell. Hell could be no more lonely or hopeless, no more agonizingly estranged from the world of order and harmony.

> I heard my voice, as though it belonged to someone else, hollow in the empty room, detached, say: "Nigger, what are you standing up there crying for?"
>
> I saw tears slick on his cheeks in the yellow light.
>
> Then I heard myself say what I have heard them say so many times. "It's not right. It's just not right."

Griffin finds a few photographic negatives in the deserted room and with "strange excitement" wonders what images are on them.

Each negative was blank.

It was another *epiphany*: the film was blank and Griffin himself had become the *Other*, cut off from his intimate self, now a bald stranger in a mirror, a cipher. He took out his notebook, to write a letter to his wife. He got as far as:

> *Hattiesburg, November 14.*
> *My darling,*

... and the words would not come. The rest of the page remained a blank.

In a phrase dating back to early Christianity, it was, for Griffin—figuratively *and* literally—a dark night of the soul.

He felt a foreboding:

> I felt disaster. Somewhere in the night's future the tensions would explode into violence. The white boys would race through too fast. They would see a man or a boy or a woman

alone somewhere along a street and the lust
to beat or to kill would flood into them. Some
frightening thing had to climax this accelerat-
ing madness.

Griffin was far more prophetic than he could have
imagined, but he wasn't the only voice: Martin Luther
King Jr. and James Baldwin were also warning of the
same consequences. One of James Baldwin's most famous books *The Fire Next Time*, was published in 1963.
Martin Luther King Jr.'s *Why We Can't Wait* was published in 1964.

In 1965, riots broke out in the Watts area of Los
Angeles, which lasted six days, August 11-15, until the
melee was subdued on the 16th. By the time the riots
ended, 34 people had been killed, 2,032 injured and
3,952 arrested. There was 440 million dollars in property damage and 977 buildings destroyed. Martial laws
had to be declared and about 2,000 members of the
the National Guard had to be mobilized. The streets of
Watts resembled a war zone. Los Angeles Police Chief
William Parker characterized participants as no more
than "monkeys in a zoo," which also fueled emotions.

A California state commission later blamed the riots
on high unemployment, poor schools and other inferior
living conditions. The government subsequently made
little effort to address the problems or repair damages.

In 1992, the Rodney King riots broke out, beginning April 29. They were sparkled by the jury acquit-
tal of four Los Angeles Police Department officers ac-
cused in the videotape beating of African-American
motorist Rodney King, following a high speed pursuit.
Thousands of people in the Los Angeles area rioted over

the six days following the verdict. At the time, similar, smaller riots and anti-police actions took place in other locations in the United States and Canada. Widespread looting, assault, arson and murder occurred, and property damage topped roughly one billion dollars. In all, 53 people died during the riots and thousands were injured.

Griffin's haphazard odyssey continued; he returned briefly to New Orleans, hitchhiked across Mississippi, to Mobile.

He applied for jobs in Mobile and was invariably turned down. He was not surprised. He got rides from white men, who invariably wanted to know about the sex life of Negro men—did they all want white women? How large was their manhood, did they have more stamina than whites?

Griffin was sickened by the conversations but had to remain evasive, polite but noncommittal.

Between Mobile and Montgomery he got a ride from "a large, pleasant-faced man" in a truck, who freely admitted he hired black women for his business and for housework—but only after they slept with him. Griffin's continued noncommittal conversation rankled the driver; he took Griffin's silence for disapproval:

> "Where you from?" he asked.
> "Texas."
> "What're you doing down here?"
> "Just traveling around, trying to finds jobs."
> "You're not down here to stir up trouble, are you?"
> "Oh, God, no."

"You start stirring up these niggers and we sure as hell know how to take care of you."

"I don't intend to."

"Do you know what we do to troublemakers down here?"

"No, sir."

"We either ship them off to the pen or kill them."

Griffin told the rest of the story, as if it had been seared into his memory:

> He spoke in a tone that sickened me, casual, merciless. I looked at him. His decent eyes turned yellow.
>
> I knew that nothing could touch him to have mercy once he decided Negroes should be "taught a lesson." The immensity of it terrified me. But it caught him up like a lust now. He entertained it, his voice unctuous with pleasure and cruelty. The highway stretched deserted through the swamp forests. He nodded toward the solid wall of brush flying past our windows.
>
> "You can kill a nigger and toss him into the swamp and no one'll ever know what happened to him."

As if by contrast, Griffin got a ride from a young Negro man; he had, Griffin learned, a wife and six children, from nine years to four months, and lived in a two-room shanty off the highway, "patched at the bottom with a Dr. Pepper sign." He was a sawmill worker, but never really got out of debt. He offered to let Griffin come to his home.

The man, wife and children shared their meal with Griffin: yellow beans cooked in water, mashed beans and canned milk for the youngest. The children ate on the floor with a newspaper as a tablecloth. Griffin gave them bread he had been carrying and treats from his duffel, Milky Way bars cut into small pieces for everyone. They all slept on pallets on the floor. The children were excited that Griffin's daughter Susie had her fifth birthday that day. They all wanted to give Mr. Griffin a hug. Griffin marveled at their welcome without qualification of any kind, and their love for one another.

When they were all asleep, Griffin went outside and quietly wept—not for being black, not for being white, but as a human parent, "for all children who had to be healed and protected, nourished and nurtured, educated and liberated."

And he wept for those six children sleeping inside the shanty, whose lives might well come to little solely because of the nature of their race.

> After breakfast of coffee and a slice of bread, we were ready to leave, I shook hands with her at the door and thanked her. Reaching for my wallet, I told her I wanted to pay her for putting me up.
>
> She refused, saying that I had brought more than I had taken. "If you gave us a penny, we'd owe you change."

Reluctantly, the wife did take Griffin's offering.

That episode, with the Negro man, his wife and six children appears to be very nearly Biblical in tone; Griffin speaks here as clearly as John Steinbeck spoke about the Joad family, in *The Grapes of Wrath*. Steinbeck's novel is clearly a retelling of the tribe of

Israel journeying from their land of bondage, Egypt, to their own promised land. But the story of the Joad family, traveling to California after being evicted from their dust bowl home and land in Oklahoma, is a black reversal of the biblical parable. The Joads find that there is no salvation in the land of oranges and sun; they are treated more savagely when they reach California than they had been in Oklahoma.

"If you gave us a penny, we'd owe you change" could have sprung intact from the pages of *The Grapes of Wrath*.

The Grapes of Wrath was first published in 1939; *Black Like Me* was published 22 years later, in 1961. No book since *The Grapes of Wrath* has so clearly revealed the agony of the lives of those marginalized and dispossessed in twentieth-century America.

Griffin reached Montgomery, Alabama, November 25. In Montgomery, he was surprised to feel the energy in the Negro community, following the passive resistance teachings of Martin Luther King Jr., who had, in turn, learned from Gandhi.

> Here, the Negro has committed himself to a definite stand. He will go to jail, suffer any humiliation, but he will not back down. He will take the insults and abuses stoically so that his children will not have to take them in the future.
>
> The white racist is bewildered and angry by such an attitude, because the dignity of the Negro's course of action emphasizes the indignity of his own.

He saw the "hate stare" everywhere.

Griffin then decided to *go back*, to become white again.

On November 28, he re-entered the white world; the shift was, he said, "nerve-wracking." Moving to and from the doppelgänger second self meant risking his entire soul, although Griffin did not quite realize that at the time.

His skin had changed to the extent that Negroes would not talk to him or even acknowledge him. He said hello to a white policeman, who nodded in return:

> I was once more a first-class citizen, that all doors to cafes, rest rooms, libraries, movies concerts, schools and churches were suddenly open to me. After so long I could not adjust to it. A sense of exultant liberation flooded through me. I crossed over to a restaurant and entered. I took a seat beside white men at the counter and the waitress smiled at me. It was a miracle. I ordered food and it was served, and it was a miracle. I went to the rest room and was not molested. No one paid me the slightest attention. No one said, "What're you doing in here, nigger?"

Inadvertently, Griffin made a horrific mistake:

> I developed a technique of zigzagging back and forth. In my bag I kept a damp sponge, dyes, cleansing cream and Kleenex. It was hazardous, but it was the only way to traverse an area both as Negro and white. As I traveled, I would find an isolated spot, perhaps an alley

at night or the brush beside a highway, and quickly apply the dye to face, hands and legs, then rub off and reapply until it was firmly anchored in my pores. I would go through the area as a Negro and then, usually at night, remove the dyes with cleaning cream and tissues and pass through the same area as a white man.

But the shifts were too costly to his psyche—he discovered it was extraordinarily exhausting to move back and forth between worlds, each with its own unspoken rules of conduct and isolation from the other.

Griffin traveled into Georgia. It was an ironic return: one former Georgia Governor Griffin (who was no relation of his, Griffin thankfully thought) earned a place in his state's history by keeping Negroes "in their place."

He scrubbed the dye off in a Atlanta bus station men's room and emerged as a white man. His odyssey was over.

Eight |

Firestorm

... he found his true métier ...

1960 – 1961
Texas

THE TWO-FACED GOD of fame and notoriety often affects writers in similar fashion, years or decades apart; writers who may anticipate fame are often blindsided by the sudden twists and torques of notoriety.

John Steinbeck was born in Salinas, California and grew up in the Salinas-Monterey Bay area. He published his epic novel, *The Grapes of Wrath* in 1939, which many now believe is the premier novel of Depression-era America, a moral vision of the 1930s. It was instantly hailed as a twentieth-century classic, but was also vilified by officials in Oklahoma and in California, Diatribes against Steinbeck were read into the Congressional Record by Oklahoma congressmen. In California, his novel was branded "obscene in the extreme" by small town politicians, a few who later admitted they hadn't even read his book before making that charge. And he was warned; he later wrote to a friend, Chase Horton:

> Let me tell you a story. When *The Grapes of Wrath* got loose, a lot of people were pretty mad at me. The undersheriff of Santa Clara County was a friend of mine and he told me as follows— "Don't you go into any hotel room alone. Keep records of every minute and when you are off the ranch travel with one or two friends and particularly, don't stay in a hotel alone." "Why?" I asked. "Maybe I'm sticking my neck out, but the boys got a rape case set up for you. You get alone in a hotel and a dame will come in, tear off her clothes, scratch her face and scream and you try to talk yourself out of that one. They won't touch your book but there's easier ways."

Steinbeck found himself constantly hounded; by well-meaning individuals who wanted interviews, by other individuals and groups who wanted him to donate his royalties to their own causes, and by outright enemies.

He fled to Mexico for a year with his friend marine biologist Ed Ricketts. They chartered a ship, the Western Flyer, and went on an extended trip to collect marine specimens in the Gulf of California, which they called by its ancient name, The Sea of Cortez. That led to a Steinbeck-Ricketts collaboration, *The Sea of Cortez*, published in 1941 and Steinbeck's own *The Log from the Sea of Cortez*, published in 1951, following Ricketts' death, when his car was hit by a train in Monterey.

The Log from the Sea of Cortez contained a long eulogy about Ricketts; perhaps the most famous eulogy in modern American literature.

After *The Grapes of Wrath* was published, Steinbeck was never again welcome in his home state of California. He drove through it during the research for his book, *Travels with Charley: In Search of America,* published in 1962; he admitted he didn't recognize his own home state. He sometimes referred to "the old hatreds," he encountered there.

He may have wanted to settle in the Monterey Bay area, with a view of the Bay. In his latter years, he found a home facing the water, but it was the other coast; he lived in Sag Harbor, Long Island, with a view of the Atlantic, not the Pacific.

Griffin traveled to Fort Worth January 2, 1960, to again meet George Levitan, publisher of *Sepia* magazine. Levitan gave him one more chance to back out of publishing the series of articles, as they originally agreed upon: "Journey into Shame."

"The only way I'll run it is if you insist," Levitan said. "Then I think we must run it," Griffin said.

By January 30, word had spread about what he had done, and he was receiving requests for television and radio interviews.

> I realize the hatred it will bring me in the South and I look on the next months with the worst possible dread. I have the deep conviction that I am on the right side—the side of justice; but it will be a dirty bath, regardless, for the

opposition refuses to reason, to debate, to seek the truth. They brand and hate, that is all.

The first article in the series was set for publication in the March 17, 1960 issue, but was later published back to the April 17 issue. His articles ran consecutively from April to Sept. 17.

Before the first article appeared Griffin was receiving death threats, by mail and on the telephone from racists in his own hometown of Mansfield, Texas.

Then the Griffin family began to keep a loaded shotgun near the front door.

He was also warned never to meet an unknown woman without witnesses because of a fraudulent rape charge. The advice could have been word-for-word the same as the warning given John Steinbeck, years earlier.

On April 2, Griffin got a call from a reporter at the *Fort Worth Star-Telegram*. Did Griffin know what happened ? He did not.

He had been hanged in effigy—a dummy was found hanging from downtown Mansfield's only stoplight. It was half black, half white, with a yellow stripe down its back. It had been taken to the town dump, where Griffin later found it. It had been placed near a sign: $25. FINE FOR DUMPING DEAD ANIMALS.

It was not a very good likeness, Griffin observed.

It was no longer safe to stay in Mansfield. His parents were more frightened than he; they made plans to sell their home and move to Mexico, where their older son Edgar owned some real estate. On August 15, 1960, they drove to Mexico. Three days later, Griffin put his wife and children on a plane for Mexico City. He packed up his car and drove to meet them soon after; they settled in a small village overlooking the Spanish colonial city of Morelia, in the Sierra Tarasca mountains, about 130 miles west of Mexico City. It was their home for nearly a year and Griffin wrote the first draft of *Black Like Me* there.

`The irony was not lost on Griffin; the first time he had been forced into exile was by the Nazis, when he fled France ahead of the Gestapo; now he was forced into exile again, this time by racists in his hometown.

Eventually, there was a series of uprisings in the Mexican town of Morelia. Griffin returned to the United States, forced to flee for the third time, this time by Mexican communists.

By then the property in Mansfield has been sold; they moved back to the cinderblock house on the Holland family farm. They subsequently moved to Fort Worth in 1967.

Black Like Me was published in August, 1961. Reviews were largely exceptional:

> In describing his encounters with Negroes and whites, Griffin not only reveals the depth of the gulf separating the races in the south but conveys the psychological impact of being inside someone else's skin.... For all of its despair the book is rooted in courage and the conviction that there must be communication between black and white.
> —*Booklist magazine,*
> *October 15, 1961*

This personal telling of the experience of segregation and second-class citizenship carries a shock and a poignancy which statistics obscure; it also reveals the human urgency which discussions of the "race problem" sometimes miss.

—*Joseph Duffy in The Christian Century, January 3, 1962*

Telling, as he does so well, what he felt during these six weeks, Griffin, the novelist, adds a dimension to his book that no mere reporter could hope to achieve with even the most impressive array of facts and figures.... It is the frankness and personal honesty of the author which raises the book high above the sensational aspect of its creation.

—*B.A. Cook in Commonweal, October 27, 1961*

All of (Griffin's) experiences were not bad, but he did find that when his unusual journalistic methods became public he and his family could no longer live in Mansfield. His book is a telling testament to the realities of race hatred.

—*Kirkus reviews, August 1, 1961*

Although the author remains surprisingly objective, he is almost brutally frank and some episodes make grim reading, but it is a book on our number one social problem which thoughtful young people should read.

—*Library Journal, May 15, 1962*

Mr. Griffin's report, in diary form, is uneven, at times ungrammatical, and based on a doubtful premise. The idea that a white man must live a Negroes life to understand his problems disregards the capacity of the white man ... to see through the evils of oppression and discrimination.... Mr. Griffin is at his best when he describes a bus ride from New Orleans to Hattiesburg shortly after the Mack Parker lynching, a hitch-hiking tour from Biloxi, Miss., to Selma, Ala., and various accounts of is fleeing contacts with whites cruelly intent on "keeping Negroes in their place".... Unfortunately, there is too little of such accounts of personal experience in Mr. Griffin's report and too much unoriginal philosophizing about "The Negro Problem."

The best that can be said is that Mr. Griffin's book represents an interesting journalistic experiment that does not yield from its promise.

—*S.H. Loory, The New York Herald Tribune, October 15, 1961*

The story of this incredible adventure (is) told here in bare, unemotional pedestrian prose which gains in its drama from its very sparseness.... We have had, in Wright and Baldwin and others, the story of how it is to be black as told by a Negro. Here we have it in reverse terms: how the shock of being black hits a white man. This is strong stuff.

—*R.J. Gleason, The San Francisco Chronicle, October 21, 1961*

This was not a stunt; this was not a lark, carried out by a free-lance writer in search of a story.... "Black Like Me" is a moving and a troubling book written by an accomplished novelist. Though slender, this volume is a scathing indictment of our society.

> —L.E. Lomax, *The Saturday Review of Literature*,
> December 9, 1961.

When the book was published in Great Britain in 1962, Cyril Connolly wrote, in *The Sunday Times of London*, "Some actions are so absolutely simple and right that they amount to genius. It was an act of genius on the part of Mr. Griffin to decide to dye his skin and live as a Negro. Why did nobody think of it before?"

Even Malcolm X mentioned *Black Like Me*. In *The Autobiography of Malcolm X*, he wrote:

> Two American authors, best-sellers in the Holy Land, had helped spread and intensify the concern for the American black man. James Baldwin's books, translated, had made a tremendous impact, as had the book *Black Like Me* by John Griffin. If you're unfamiliar with that book, it tells how the white man Griffin blackened his skin and spent two months traveling as a Negro about America; then Griffin wrote of the experiences that he met. "A frightening experience!" I heard exclaimed many times by people in the Holy World who had read the popular book. But I never heard it without opening their thinking further: "Well, if it was a frightening experience for him as nothing but a make-believe Negro for sixty days—then you think about what *real* Negroes in America have gone through for four hundred years."

Except for newspapers in Atlanta, and one in Hattiesburg, Mississippi, where publisher P.D. East was a personal friend of Griffin's, *Black Like Me* was ignored in the south.

Black Like Me was never planned to be a first-person diary. Griffin originally planned it as a dry, sociological study, but his emotions intruded. As he wrote in the Preface;

> This began as a scientific research study of the Negro in the south, with careful compilation of data for analysis. But I filed the data, and here publish the journal of my own experience living as a Negro. I offer it in all its crudity and rawness. It traces the changes that occur to heart and body and intelligence when the so-called first-class citizen is cast on the junk heap of second- class citizenship.

(His editor at Houghton Mifflin, Gerta Kennedy, asked that this past paragraph be deleted because it was too strong. Griffin refused.)

The power of *Black Like Me* comes, in large part, from the intense emotions in the book. In fact, Griffin's emotions permeate the book. Reading it now, 50 years after it was first published does not diminish its intensity. Griffin's first-person "I" speaks directly to each reader. It is as powerful now as it was when it was first published because of how Griffin reveals himself:

> October 28, 1959:
> I was prepared to walk into a life that appeared suddenly to be mysterious and frightening.

October 29:

I felt the beginning loneliness, the terrible dread of what I decided to do.

November 7:

The transformation total and shocking. I had expected to see myself disguised, but this was something else. I was imprisoned in the flesh of an utter stranger, an unsympathetic one with whom I felt no kinship. All traces of the John Howard Griffin I had been were wiped from existence. Even the senses underwent a change so profound it filled me with distress.

November 8:

My flesh prickled with shame....

November 10-12:

I left, sick with exhaustion, wondering where a Negro could sit to rest.

November 14:

I knew I was receiving what the Negroes call "the hate stare." It my first experience with it. It is far more than a look of disapproval one occasionally gets. This was so exaggerating hateful....

And on, throughout Griffin's journey.

When *Black Like Me* was first published in hardcover, the Houghton Mifflin edition sold 100,000 copies.

By the end (of 1961), *Black Like Me* had been published in England and Canada to excellent reviews and the book had been distributed in fifty-eight English-speaking countries. At the same time it had been translated into French, German and Polish and was well-received in Europe. (It would go on to be a two-million-copy best-seller in France, where it remains in print after thirty-five years. Signet brought out the paperback edition in late 1962, and it would sell over five million copies during the decade (of the 1960s).

Eventually it was published in England, France, Germany, Italy, Holland and sixty other countries in thirteen languages, selling ten million copies worldwide. Portions of the book appeared in anthologies, magazines and newspapers. It continues to be excerpted as a text in the areas of sociology, race relations, psychology, investigative journalism, spiritual humanism, education and literature.

In 1962 a black and white movie was made of the book, starring James Whitmore. It was—as has been said of countless other productions—a movie only Hollywood could love. Or, in one word: lurid. Carl Lerner, a former film editor, was directing his first film.

Typical of how the movie was received was a review that Judith Crist published in *The New York Herald Tribune* May 21, 1964:

'Black Like Me'
—Noble Intent,
Vulgar Effect

"Black Like Me" is a good-will gesture gone wrong—gone so far wrong in form and content, in fact, that its high purpose and noble intent are all but perverted. Fortunately, at least for those concerned with furthering the cause of the Negro and interracial understanding, its thesis is so lacking in credibility and its dramatization so vulgar where it is not banal that we may presume the film will have minimal audience influence.

She also wrote:

> Both white and Negro characters he encounters are super-stereotypes, from Will Geer's red neck to Eva Jessy's "mammy," and while they jar the ear, neither slang nor four-letter words can disguise the triteness of the dialogue; sharp cutting and the labored insertion of arty slum or naive shots fail to relieve the tedium of the episode-and-flashback routine and Meyer Kupferman's score, bristling with portent, serves only to underline the banality and cheap sensationalism of the script.
>
> The seriousness and good intent of those involved in the film cannot be denied, but the incredible mixture of sex, sociology they have come up with smacks with opportunism and ineptitude.

Whitmore, who had the general build of Griffin, played the role of "John Finley Horton" with an unceasing anger, exactly the wrong emotion, Griffin observed:

> He played it angry all the way through. I couldn't behave that way when I was doing it in real life. I'd have been killed. But Whitmore became so outraged, he couldn't control himself.

The film is hard to find these days, and probably just as well; it cannot possibly be viewed as any accurate example of Griffin's experiences.

When *Black Like Me* was published Griffin found his true *métier*; he would never again publish a novel during his lifetime. *Street of the Seven Angels*, written while he was blind, was published posthumously, 23 years after his death, in 2003.

He became an activist, a liberal in the best sense of that word, and in the years thereafter gave over 1,100 lectures and presentations about civil rights and race relations.

Both Steinbeck and Griffin avoided any possible rape charges, but one night in Mississippi, in 1975, almost 15 years after the first publication of *Black Like Me*, the Klu Klux Klan trapped Griffin on a dark deserted road and attacked him with chains.... Griffin remembers hearing "... get his kidneys...."

The beating was brutal and he was left for dead. He sustained permanent kidney damage but did not speak of the incident publicly.

(One question is left unanswered here: why did Griffin go back into the vicious heart of the racist south—apparently alone—even years after publication of *Black Like Me*, when he might have known he would still be at physical risk? The ultimate answer: after all those years, he simply let his guard down, assuming nothing would happen....)

He was not deterred; he continued to speak out. He could not do otherwise.

Nine |

The Church and the Black Man

"The book achieved immediate obscurity ..."

1960s
Texas

THE DECADE OF THE 1960s was Griffin's most productive years; with unending lectures, appearances and publications.

Black Like Me was followed by an anthology of his work up through the late '60s: Bradford Daniel edited a large volume of Griffin's work, titled *The John Howard Griffin Reader*, published in 1968. The 600-page collection included Daniel's abridgment of Griffin's first two novels, portions of *Black Like Me* and *Land of the High Sky*, a group of six short stories, a folio of Griffin's photographic portraits (of Maxwell Geismar, Thomas Merton, Jacques Maritain, Pierre Reverdy, Saul Alinsky and others) and a selection of works in progress. This section featured chapters from the book subsequently published as *Scattered Shadows*, essays on music, Mexico and censorship. With an Introduction by Maxwell Geismar, *The Reader* introduced Griffin's other work to a much wider audience and the volume sold over 39,000 cloth copies.

But, Griffin later said, *Black Like Me* had two glaring weaknesses: first, the journey had been limited to the segregated south; second, he had omitted criticism of religious institutions.

Griffin could have gone back to Texas after his sojourn in the south, re-set his mental and psychological gyroscope and gone into the north as a black man; that part would have been logical— several years later Grace Halsell became black, worked in Harlem then traveled to the south and worked as a domestic servant. That part, for Griffin, would have been workable.

But how he could have worked essays into *Black Like Me* about deficiencies in organized religion about treatment of Negroes is more problematic. His first person I-form diary would not have allowed Griffin any area or section to discuss religion without breaking the narrative, unless he could have possibly added essays at the end of the book as a postscript.

> I did not write about the churches for two reasons.
>
> First, I was so deeply shocked to be driven away from churches that would have welcomed me at any time as a white man that I did not know how to handle this and I feared I might be committing an injustice. Second, in my naiveté, I was certain that as soon as these conditions were made known to church leadership, the matter would be corrected.

But, as Robert Bonazzi wrote:

> instead of stimulating any changes, he
> heard outright denials and dubious rational-
> izations from white priests and bishops. He
> was told that Negro Catholics, for instance,
> preferred their own churches, especially in the
> South. In other regions, where churches had
> been desegregated, he was told that black pa-
> rishioners understood why it was best to take a
> pew at the back and let the whites take commu-
> nion first. The white clergy indicated that black
> people wanted it that way. However, when he
> spoke with black parishioners, they said that
> these practices had not been due to their pref-
> erence, but that they accepted them out of re-
> spect for the churches.

Since his first journey to France, Griffin had read
all the major theologians and religious philosophers of
the twentieth-century, especially Catholic theologians,
and in his later years had deep personal friendship
with many, including Thomas Merton and French philosopher Jacques Maritain.

He called Thomas Merton, who was aware of the situation, and Merton urged Griffin to pursue his convictions. Biographer Robert Bonazzi said Merton's words
were, for Griffin, a Catholic, almost a command to his
personal vow of obedience.

Griffin then wrote an essay, "Racist Sins of
Christians," which was published in the August 1963
issue of *The Sign*, the leading Catholic magazine of the
day.

That led to his meeting with a young priest from
Louisiana, August Thompson. His essay "Dialogue with

Father August Thompson" was published in *Ramparts* magazine.

Father Thompson made the accusation "in some areas, we Negro priests might be called second-class Christs, if that's possible." Thompson's bishop attempted to censor the interview.

Griffin certainly got the publicity—and headlines—he wanted about the issue:

> "Negro priests says segregation makes second-class citizens"
> — *The New York Times*

> "Fear and Faith in the Deep South"
> — *The San Francisco Chronicle*

> "Negro Priest says segregated church exists in the south"
> — *The Catholic Messenger*

In 1969, Griffin published *The Church and the Black Man*. It was a most unusual book; it was published by the small publishing firm, Pflaum Press of Dayton, because, as Robert Bonazzi writes, "no establishment publisher would risk being associated with such radical views at the time." It was oversized—eight and one half inches by eleven inches—and carried the odd notation "as seen by John Howard Griffin," as only about sixty percent of the text was his.

In a paper envelope, inside the back cover of the book was a bright, flimsy, double-sided red record (presumably 45 rpm) "SOUNDS OF *The Church and the Black Man* IN AMERICA"

The first side contained: Band 1, Rev. James Groppi, *Pacem in Terris* address, Davenport, Iowa; Band 2, Rev. Albert Cleage, addressing the Black Priests' Caucus, Detroit, Michigan. Side two of the record was a continuation of Rev. Cleage's address. The oversized book and the flimsy bright red record cost $2.95. Many surviving copies of *The Church and the Black Man* no longer include the record, lost in the intervening years.

Griffin writes, in the opening chapter, "The Church and the Black Man":

> On Passion Sunday, 1968, Dick Gregory and I walked with the campus minister toward the chapel of the University of the Pacific in Stockton, California. The minister briefed us on our schedules for the day. Dick Gregory would speak at the morning worship service in the campus chapel and I would speak that afternoon at Mass in a nearby all-white community.
> Dick Gregory glanced up at the sunlit facade of the chapel.
> "God I hate to go in these pagan temples of hypocrisy," he said.
> Neither of us answered. There was nothing to answer. I remembered a scene in the kitchen of St. Catherine's rectory in Chicago where we talked through the night with a group of priests serving slum parishes. Dick Gregory told how, as a youngster, he had sought refuge in Catholic churches. "I'd open the door and look in. If the church was empty, I'd go in and sit—just to get away from the noise and stink of the slum—just to be alone for awhile away from all that."

Now, the kinds of edifices he had once considered places of sanctuary had become in his mind "pagan temples of hypocrisy."

They listened that Sunday to a liturgy that struck them as starkly personal.

"O God, sustain my cause, give me redress against a race that knows no piety, save me from a treacherous and cruel foe ..."

... and, in a chapter, "Some Painful Truths":

> We have lived under two damaging delusions in this land. First, the delusion of southern white man that we knew everything about what we patronizingly called "our Negroes," and that no outsider could possibly understand.
>
> Second, the delusion in nonsouthern areas that "it's not like that here."
>
> We still hear widespread expressions of both delusions. These expressions come from perfectly sincere white man. No black man believes either of them, of course. The experience of blackness gives lie to both delusions.
>
> The patterns of such delusions are clearer in the south and they shed light on the more complex ones of nonsouthern areas.

... and ...

> We were told that only "white trash" would be unkind to black people. And "good whites" we had to understand that "our Negroes" were just racially and ethnically different from us, childlike and "inferior," through no fault of their

own, and we had to understand and love them as they were, all in taking certain precautions to keep them in their place.

As white children we were dimly aware that the trash did frightful things to black men and woman. We heard rumors about the sexual mutilation of black men at lynchings. We heard about the large crowds that sometimes attended public lynchings, about mothers who held their children above the crowd for a good view. The delusion that we were not prejudiced was strengthened in us because most of us were not at such lynchings; we were in our homes, hearing our parents and grandparents lament such monstrousness.

We failed to perceive the obvious: that racism had dehumanized the racist even more than it had dehumanized his victims, that the racist himself was clearly racism's most tragic victim.

... and, in the chapter, "The Good White":

Ten years ago a great reservoir of *a priori* forgiveness existed in the black world. Black men still spoke of "the good white" with affection, hope and gratitude.

The "good white" was that man or woman in the community who gave some evidence of concern for truth and justice and who appeared to understand that things were not right. The good white—the minister, teacher, doctor, lawyer, newsman or housewife—somehow got the message back to black men: although they could not do much at the moment because of reprisals from their own white community, when the time came, they would be the ones to stand up for truth and justice. Good whites, usually religiously identifiable men and women, were a safety valve of hope. They were silent, but they were known by black men in each community.

In the black world we talked about such persons, identified them. "They can't do much now, but when the time comes ..."

Even before the time came, a handful spoke out and took the consequences. Lillian Smith, the great Clarence Jordan, newsman P.D. East and others. They stood as heroic symbols of "the good white." Archbishop Rummel and later Archbishop Hallinan spoke and acted at a time when it took great courage, and they did it without equivocation. They reinforced the black man's belief in "the good white."

Then the "time" came: Little Rock, Clinton, Mansfield and other cities where racism flared openly.

With rare exceptions, the "good whites" on whom black people counted, remained silent and invisible.

No one wanted to listen to Griffin advise or perhaps harass them about the failings of the church. In two memorable phrases by Robert Bonazzi, *The Church and the Black Man* "fell on deaf white ears" and "the book achieved immediate obscurity."

Ten |

A Time to Be Human

"My first vivid memory of life...."

1977
Texas

WHEN HIS EYESIGHT RETURNED, Griffin over-com-pensated; his first draft of *Land of the High Sky* ex-ceeded 1,300 pages. He also overcompensated upon his return to the visual world by becoming an accom-plished black-and-white photographer.

The Church and the Black Man, published in 1969, was the first of four text-and-photographs books Griffin published in five years.

He followed that with *A Hidden Wholeness: The Visual World of Thomas Merton*, in 1970; *Twelve Photographic Portraits*, in 1973 and *Jacques Maritain: Homage in Words and Pictures* in 1974.

His last book on racism, *A Time to be Human*, was published in 1977. It also included black-and-white photographs: a striking double-page picture of Holocaust victims, including a young child with arms raised in surrender; a Negro sharecropper and his two children, an *everyman* photograph, but which might well have been the man with the six children who took Griffin into his shanty in *Black Like Me*.

Other photographs included a portrait of Griffin himself, bearded, gazing placidly into the camera lens; a double-page picture of a Klu Klux Klan rally and a picture of a young Negro woman with a sign that simply reads: JUSTICE.

He begins with an anecdote which could be familiar to Griffin readers:

> My first vivid memory of life begins with the word "nigger." As a very small child I used that word in speaking to a black man in my grandfather's grocery store in south Dallas. I had scarcely spoken when I was jolted by a hard slap across my face and by the anger in my grandfather's voice as he snapped, "They're people—don't you ever let me hear you call them niggers again."
>
> In preparing this book, the memory of that incident emerged fresh again. But it could just as well have happened yesterday or this morning because the world is still full of children who learn contemptuous terms for other people, and who use them and who go on being formed by them.

It was, in large part, a simple paean for understanding and a self-examination of how the experience of *Black Like Me* had affected him, sixteen years previously:

The deepest shock I experienced as a black man was the realization that everything is utterly different when one is the victim of racial prejudice.

Griffin repeated an anecdote he had written about in *The Church and the Black Man*, the well-attended lynching when women held their children high so they could witness it. In his previous version he did not mention the locale. The location was only 90 miles from Griffin's home. The lynching was delayed for three days, Griffin writes,

> so they could bring in special tourist trains for people who wanted to watch it. Two thousand tourists—men, women and children—flocked into that town of Waco, Texas.

Readers can almost visualize Griffin cringing at the memory. The victim was burned at the stake, he wrote. Worse yet, if there could possibly be a *worse yet*, everyone soon discovered the mob had killed an innocent man.

Griffin also returned to his concept of the *Other*, which he had previously discussed in a variety of circumstances:

> In Nazi Germany the non-Jewish child was brought up to view Jewish people as the "other." In Ireland today the Protestant child is taught to believe that the Catholic child is "other," and the Catholic child is taught to see the Protestant child as "other." We find the same pattern when

we hear people refer to the French as "immoral" or to the Mexicans as "lazy," or to any group as possessing "racial characteristics" of a degrading nature. And once we believe that a group of people is "different" then we can believe that they do not need or deserve the same rights and liberties we always claim for ourselves.

And he cites two quotations from Edmund Burke: "I know of no way of drawing up an indictment against a whole people" and, later, "All that is required for the triumph of evil is simply that good men remain silent long enough."

Griffin's conclusion:

It seems to me that this is the key to the racist fallacy. The Nazis had drawn up an indictment against the entire Jewish community. Once that indictment had been drawn—and far more important, once men had consented to it and did not immediately cry "No!"—the rest followed.

In *Black Like Me*, Griffin writes about Sterling Williams, the Negro shoeshine man in New Orleans. Once Williams was let in on Griffin's secret, they spoke in hushed, conspiratorial tones: two black men, speaking almost in whispers about *how to be black*.

In *A Time to Be Human*, Griffin reveals that his naivete occasionally took him one further step toward the absurd:

Since segregation was total in those days, with few hotels for black people, I had to take rooms in the homes of black people whenever I traveled.

I would usually manage this by going into a community and asking the name of a local black minister who would know a great many people. I would ask him to recommend some family that might have a room I could occupy.

But I could not stay in the homes of black people under false pretenses, so I would try to tell my hosts the truth. I would say, "Before I can accept your shelter and the food from your table, I have to tell you a truth about myself that might surprise you." They would look at me expectantly and then I would announce, "I am not really a black man. I am a white man."

The looks of pain and distress in the eyes of my hosts told me clearly what they were too courteous to say in words. Their looks said, "Now I wonder what the preacher is doing saddling us with this big black man who thinks he's white."

He did not discuss statistics in *Black Like Me*, but he offered an update in *A Time to Be Human*:

In 1975, this country had a national unemployment figure of 7.9 percent, but one out of every four employable blacks was unemployed—25 percent. For every 100 black children under 18, 42.7 lived in poverty in 1975, whereas for every 100 white children under 18, only 14.9 lived in poverty. And the gap in median income between black and white families has actually widened in the ten years between 1965 and 1975. In 1965 the average black

family had $59 in purchasing power for every
$100 available to the white family; in 1975 it
was $57.

Toward the end of *A Time to Be Human*, Griffin
writes:

> What suppressed minorities the world over
> have learned is that the racism directed against
> them *has little or nothing to do with what they
> do or fail to do*, that discrimination against
> them does not depend on them but on the politi-
> cal and economic climate as a whole. Today, the
> deepest frustration of minorities comes from
> this fact. They are being blamed for conditions
> which they in no way caused.

Racism was never a closed chapter in Griffin's life;
he never expected to see the end of racism in his lifetime. But he never published another book about it.
Perhaps he didn't need to. By the time *A Time to Be
Human* was released, late in his life, *Black Like Me* was
in print throughout much of the world.

Eleven |

The Merton Years:
The Hermitage Journals

oh ye of little faith ...

August, 1969–June, 1972
Texas and Gethsemani Abbey,
Kentucky

THOMAS MERTON WAS ARGUABLY the most influential American Catholic author of the twentieth-century. He was born in France, in 1915, moved to the United States and became a Catholic while attending Columbia University.

In December, 1941, he entered the Abbey of Gethsemani, in Kentucky, a community of Trappist monks. He spent twenty-seven years in Gethsemani and those years "brought about profound changes in his self-understanding. This ongoing conversation impelled him into the political arena, where be became, according to Daniel Berrigan, the conscience of the peace movement of the 1960s. Referring to race and peace as the two most urgent issues of our time, Merton was a

strong supporter of the nonviolent civil rights movement, which he called 'certainly the greatest example
of Christian faith in action in the social history of the
United States.'"

For his social activism, Merton endured severe criticism from all sides, Catholics and non-Catholics alike.

Merton wrote over seventy books. His autobiography, *The Seven Storey Mountain* (1948) has sold over
one million copies and has been translated into over fifteen languages.

Some of his books were: *Man in the Divided Sea*
(1946); *The Ascent to Truth* (1951); *The Last of the
Fathers* (1954); *No Man Is an Island* (1955); *The
Living Bread* (1956); *Thoughts in Solitude* (1958); *The
Secular Journal of Thomas Merton*; *Selected Poems*
(1959); *Gandhi on Non-Violence* (1965).

Merton died December 10, 1968, at 53, in Bangkok,
Thailand, where he had spoken at an interfaith meeting
between Roman Catholic and non-Christian monks. He
was electrocuted when he touched a live electric cord
after leaving a bath.

Publications of his work did not end with his death.
Posthumous publications included: *Contemplation in a
World of Action* (1971); *The Asian Journal of Thomas
Merton* (1973); *The Collected Poems of Thomas Merton*
(1977); *Love and Living* (1979); and other titles, up
through *The Cold War Letters*, published in 2006.

He was, clearly, the most prolific monk in American
Catholicism; he was also a priest and the first Cistercian
hermit since the middle ages.

He was a proponent of interfaith understanding and
began dialogues with the Dalai Lama, D.T. Suzuki, the

Japanese writer on the Zen tradition and others.

John Howard Griffin was appointed by the Merton Legacy Trust in 1969, to be the official biographer of Merton. As Conger Beasley Jr. writes, in the Introduction to Griffin's *The Hermitage Journals*: "The choice was a good one. Griffin, a Catholic convert, was a great admirer of Merton and a close personal friend. At first, Griffin did not want the job; he would be required to read Merton's voluminous personal journals, which he was reluctant to do out of respect for such an intensely private man."

But Griffin agreed to the job; and from 1969 into 1971, he drove from Texas to the Kentucky monastery, where he spent a week or ten days, before returning home. He made eighteen visits, from August, 1969 to June, 1972.

Merton and Griffin had much in common; Merton was born in France; Griffin had studied there and was a Francophile. Both were converts to Catholicism, Merton was a Trappist, Griffin became a Third Order Carmelite. Both loved Gregorian chants; both became exceptional photographers in their latter days; both kept journals for decades and both were highly prolific writers.

Both shared a love of the cloistered life, a life of deep meditation and both were social activists.

> "Griffin and Merton became significant voices in the critical dialogues of their day regarding human rights, racism, war and peace, spiritual renewal, charitable love in a climate of hatred, and the survival of the environment. They attacked cultural stereotypes,

technological icons, political oppression, mass media message and stupidity in general. They combined sophisticated discourse, ethical judgment, and personal in sight into a vision that vibrated with hope against absurdity. They shared a keen perspective that allowed for radical innovations in the larger context of tradition. They were open to the processes of social and interior change, scrutinizing both the images and realities of society and self. They continued to grow beyond the superficial contradictions of their points of view, always in quest of universal truths that might ignite the fires of justice and, simultaneously, calm the ego with profound humility," Robert Bonazzi wrote.

And, he wrote,

"Their work made them controversial figures, but their true vocation to solitude and creativity, to contemplation and prayer, never waned—despite social crises, critical indignation from various quarters, voluminous correspondences and poor health. Each artist endured fame and suffered from his 'public image.'"

Griffin very much wanted to live and work in Merton's footsteps; Griffin lived alone in a small cinderblock cabin deep inside the monastery grounds and he kept Merton's schedule. Up at 3:00 a.m, observances of morning offices (services), chores, lunch, more work, observances of evening offices, then to bed by 8 or 9 p.m.

And always Griffin kept journals. The purpose of his Gethsemani journals was two-fold. One: surface observations of the daily routine, people he met, Merton material to study and the daily minutiae of researching Merton's legacy. The second, and vastly more important aspect of Griffin's journals, was to become invisible himself, to be simply a conduit of Merton's life, an amanuensis of Merton's psyche.

Merton lived in solitude in Gethsemani not to find Christ, but because that was where Christ wanted to find him, he once said. The same could be true of Griffin.

Griffin's journals begin August 5, 1969, with just a brief mention that he has arrived after two days of driving from Texas. In his daily journals he mentions his illnesses, but only mentions them. These are excerpts from his *Hermitage Journals*:

> August 6, 1969
> 5:45 a.m. Before dawn. Even this quiet typewriter motor sounds an ungodly racket in the silence that possesses the countryside. I have coffee heating on the hotplate. Slept well and profoundly.
>
> 8:30 a.m. Begin to read the Asian journal, sitting on the porch. Fascinating. It warms up quickly. Sense of the hermitage, of that isolation. But part of that sense is destroyed by the sight of that car parked at the side—a way of leaving, of making quick contact with the world. It is a line that keeps things open and isolation less perfect to the senses. I cannot

walk—so on foot, if I depended on that, I could not go anywhere—thus the isolation is total. So, finally, irritated at myself for being so irritated by the sight of a car here at the hermitage, I drove it around the back, out of sight. And now the illusion of being alone, of being cut off from contact, is restored and the irritation gone. A great need to sense the isolation to the fullest.

3:45 p.m. Then I read the excellent account in French by Dom Jean Leclercq. In describing Tom's last days there, he mentioned that after his death, Tom was returned to the U.S. in a jet carrying the bodies of dead soldiers from Vietnam. "... le paradoxe de son retoru a son pays dans un 'jet' qui ramenait les corps de jeunes soldats tues en cette guarre du Vietnam dont il avait luimeme tant souffert." ("... the paradox of his return to his country in jet which was bring back the bodies of young soldiers killed in this Vietnamese war from which he suffered so much.")

August 9, 1969

The sense of loneliness is gone. In its place there is a growing reliance on the solitude and the silence (of natural sounds), and these things serve merely as the background for the intimate preoccupation of the Christ that Tom sought in the silence, of the Christ that surrounded as the silence surrounds: and out of that a tremendous enthusiasm and vitality that fills the hours, even the hours of contemplation, with a flow and rhythm that stimulates everything and reconciles superbly the realities of the body's needs with the needs of the spirit, the mind. This is one of things that made Tom unshockable in the face of any reality.

What I am trying to say, without quite knowing how, is that there is really no sense of need now to do a lot of interviews with Tom's friends. I will, of course, because that is part of it, but where before I thought it important, and felt that from such such interviews I would learn indispensable truths about Tom, I become aware that I am learning them from Tom and Tom's surroundings ... almost intuitively ...

August 12, 1969

3:00 p.m. Since the days of my old and horrible nightmares following the *Black Like Me* experience, I have never had any dreams vivid enough to recall. But last night, after reading far too late, questing, questioning, mediating, seeking to grasp these things about Tom, I finally went into a deep sleep and had the most startling and vivid dream about St. John of the Cross all mixed up with Tom's presence. I saw them both in a silent kaleidoscope changing set of patterns, like a cubist painting of great brilliance. Neither of them seemed aware of the other's presence; but they were combined: St. John of the Cross would have Tom's legs, or a hand with the scar, or Tom would have St. John's profile staring out of the side of Tom's head, where his ear ought to have been. It was, or seemed to be, prolonged. My reaction was neither ` fear nor joy, but tremendous astonishment and a fascination that glued all my concentration on them and made me really unaware of myself. It was a mounting thing until it finally woke me up, and I remember staring into the darkness of that room and telling myself out loud with a groan: "You're concentrating too much on it. You're working too relentlessly on it."

I am preoccupied about these work journals. I need to put in a great deal of material and speculation that I as the biographer alone am authorized to see. (At least for many years, and some things forever. Since the materials are so vast, I must have them, the excerpted portions at least, here to draw upon, and to document—without actually revealing them—later if the need be. And yet they must not be seen by others, probably ever. I must perhaps get a small safe in which to keep them. People are too indiscreet. The very word *confidential* marked on the documents or journals is an open invitation to some spirits to go immediately and directly *there*.)

September 17, 1969

4:45 a.m. I am terribly preoccupied by the news yesterday Father Dan Walsh ... sent me yesterday through Brother Pat. I am apparently to receive the letter today from Monsignor Horrigan (the president of Bellarmine College, in Louisville, Kentucky) about receiving the doctorate in a big ceremony in November, along with Ethel Kennedy. When this came up before I begged Brother Patrick to discourage it. I am deeply embarrassed by such things.

How can I refuse without seeming to refuse support of those things that I support with all my heart?

What I do not support is this kind of honor accorded to me (although such honors should be accorded others). It is profoundly against my grain. I will ride it a bit, see if I can gracefully find a way out of it; if not, then just accept it with as good grace as possible.

Griffin refers to his "wounds" but without specification. They were, in fact, benign tumors on his feet, a condition which he said he inherited from his father. He had this condition from the mid-1950s until his death. These made using a wheelchair at the monastery quite sensible.

September 19, 1969
4:30 and cold.

Now I have to get up and do the things of morning— bathe and dress the wounds, which get worse and not better, brush my teeth, take the medication and make up the bed.

Later: Bother Patrick found some wide gauze, which reminds me that the other day, when I began bleeding again, I asked if they could find wide gauze to bring up. Brother Richard brought up a few rolls of narrow (one inch) gauze and some tape, handed it to me and asked: "Will that be enough, John?" I looked at that tape, and looked at him and then back to the tape, and he began to turn absolutely crimson as he realized all the implications. I set the gauze on the table, turning my back to him and muttering, "Hell, that wouldn't have been big enough when I was two years old." but he didn't get that as he was saying in that soft and gentle voice: "It was the largest they had."

October 11, 1969
Saturday

Later—5 p.m. I am aware that in addition to doing the very best work here that can be done on this book—the most concentrated and sustained—I am also privileged to live some of the highest moments of my life, of my interior life. This hermit-existence, which in no way nullifies or reduces my family existence, is deeply and profoundly tasted in all its rarity.

October 13, 1969

Later. It is the happiest work I have ever done in my life, the most satisfying, the deepest adventure. *Black Like Me* was crushing and depressing as a lived experience. *Hermit Like Me* is enthralling as a lived adventure. More than enthralling ...

November 5, 1969
Wednesday.

Late evening. Cannot resist this quote from *The Geography of Lograire*, that amazing final poetic work of Thomas Merton:

So Christ went down to stay with them Niggers and took his place with them at table. He said to them, "It is very simple, much more simple than you can imagine." They replied, "You have become a white man and it is not so simple at all."

February 24, 1970

Back in the hermitage and to work after too long an absence from this blessed place. I have been to Europe, got back home a week ago, and arrived here today for a good long stay of at least ten days. It is terrible to say, but there are only two places where I am truly at home, where I want to be, where I am completely happy and right: within the rooms of my own home with my wife and children, and here in the solitude of this hermitage at Gethsemani. Only these two places. In all others, no matter how pleasant or enjoyable, I am not at home; I am vaguely miserable.

April 25, 1970
Sunday afternoon.
But I ache all over, and most distressing of all, my feet are completely numb—something off with the diabetes. They are numb, and the lower legs up nearly to the knees have no feeling at all. Will try to take a little walk and perhaps restore some of the circulation. It is beautiful, hazed and thinly overcast, the temperature up to seventy degrees—dogwoods and redbuds in bloom all through the woods.

May 16, 1970
Went to Connecticut—twenty-four hours in Hartford, twenty-four more with Nell Dorr (photographer) in Washington, Connecticut. Extremely hot. Stayed soaked all the time. Came to Louisville on the thirteenth, came out here early the fourteenth. When I arrived at the gatehouse, there were three emergency calls. One from Philadelphia. The schools (high schools) are anticipating a "race war" among black and white students at the beginning of the school year. They asked me to spend the first week of school giving conferences to students in all the schools to try to calm things and

turn the tide. Great God. I could not say no, but I did not say yes either. I said that if the situation really did develop, I would not refuse, but that I would not come unless they felt a real emergency existed.

And then Chicago called with the same damned thing. I told them I had promised Philadelphia the first week or ten days and they wanted the second. I told them the same.

I cannot go out and do all this. Two or three appearances a day for twenty days consecutively is more than I can handle physically. We will see. I cannot say no to such requests if there is a real need, either.

Following Griffin's experiences in the Second World War, he was eligible for medals and veteran's benefits. He neither requested nor accepted any medals and never requested veteran's benefits. He seldom referred to his 39 months of military service in the South Pacific. In fact, he became a pacifist.

May 21, 1970
Thursday.

Turned on the weather—to be hot and clear. Also heard that Nixon has ordered the flag flown at half-mast all day (rather than the usual half day) for the boys "who gave their lives in Vietnam." Why doesn't he tell the truth? Their lives were taken from them, in most cases at least. There was always an irony to me in this "giving one's life" when if you did not, in the army, you were shot as a deserter or something else. That is why I never took any of the medals in World War II. It is a peculiar sort of bravery when a man obeys orders, often against his grain, with the knowledge that if he does not, he gets it from his own beloved country—imprisonment, death or dishonorable discharge.

June 30, 1970
Tuesday.

Now I hear the truck coming through the woods, so I had better get some pants on. I am sitting here in tee shirt and underpants because of the terrific heat of today. The wheelchair is an enormous help. I have nothing like the pain of the past weeks and it is because I spent part of the day in the chair, which permits me to go right on working and it is a much better solution than the bed. Today is the first day I have really felt great and really worked well. The heat is fascinating. It fascinated Tom who referred to it often. It does strange things, brings a strange kind of joy to the life of the forest, to the hermit life. It is very uncomfortable, almost suffocating, but you feel a deep kinship with the panting foxes and squirrels and rabbits that seek the shade, and you hear the oboe tones of locusts in the trees as even the birds fall silent in such burning heat.

July 3, 1970. Griffin is at work, typing, sitting in his wheelchair with his feet on the footpads, when a sudden bolt of lightning surges through the cabin's electric lines, through his electric typewriter and knocks him onto the floor, the wheelchair on top of him. He later believes the rubber tires of the wheelchair saved his life. He suffers some short-term memory loss. The lightning strike knocked out all telephone service for the monastery. He not only has to continue to take medicine for his diabetes, but also medicines for muscle spasms and pain from the lightning strike. The memory loss frightens him because he can't remember if he had taken dymelor for his diabetes and he can't risk over-dosing on it. The experience gives him a deeper insight into the accidental electrocution of Thomas Merton:

> Fascinating, in a way, that my first involun-tary reaction was a loud scream, like the one Tom gave. This makes me feel absolutely cer-tain that the shock killed him, and not that he had a heart attack and fell against the fan. I feel a strange, almost tender union with him now in that moment of the jolt, the scream, the black-out and death. I returned from the momentary black-out, but he did not.

> July 10
> While shaving I allowed the thought to come and remain a moment before reject-ing it. Why did God allow me to live after that electric shock? One should not entertain such speculation for a moment, because there is no way whatsoever of thinking with God's mind in this. I cannot help but suspect, however, that perhaps it is because of the work to be done on Tom's biography, which, if it can be done prop-erly, is a work of great potential importance. It conforms in me at least, in a sense, my intuition that this must be something other than a "criti-cal evaluation," and more like an exposition (a la Beethoven); that I must take in, absorb within me everything I can, understand every-thing I can, and then allow and trust that what filters back out is as near the truth as I can get.

Griffin never completed the major biography of Merton he intended. His health was a primary reason; his diabetes was under control while he was at Gethsemani, but progressively worsened. But yet again, Griffin may well have thought himself unequal to the task; that Merton's spirituality so far surpassed Griffin's that Griffin could not attempt to capture Merton. The man who had the moral courage to become a black man and travel throughout the south to expose racism may have lacked a different will. On July 10, 1970, he also wrote:

> I feel utterly unequal to the task. I trust that the prayers of all his friends and mine, on which I count, will help me obtain the guidance of the Holy Sprit in all this. And I trust most of all that Tom will guide me. In other words, left to my own pitiful resources I could not hope to do it; but I long ago stopped counting on those for anything.
>
> People constantly ask me: "How are you going about writing the biography? What new things have you discovered about Merton? What are you studying about him now?" I give very poor answers, because the questions embarrass me. I absorb his journals and letters and writings, yes, but they are only part of it. What sense would it make to most if I told what I feel to be the truth; I listen to the silences he loved, I let the view of a tree saturate me, I let the hours before dawn pump all their silent musical jubilance into me. I light a fire in the winter. That is important. I listen to the rain and wipe up the spots where it leaks in. And that is important.

Griffin echoes the pleasure that all authors experience seeing a completed book for the first time:

> Sept. 1970
> Saturday
>
> Later—after lunch. Brother Patrick brought up the big envelope containing the bound edition of *A Hidden Wholeness.* He insisted I open it and get the first look.
>
> I never saw him so excited. We went through it page by page. Beautiful simple, unornamented. He was thrilled by the jacket, which I had seen, and both of us were delighted with the binding and the calligraph on the cover. Significantly our first sight of the book is here in the hermitage—the first bound and finished copy lies here on the desk in Thomas Merton's cabin. The book offers me a unique and quiet sense of satisfaction. I am glad it exists, and grateful that it exists in such a beautiful and tasteful presentation. The layout is extraordinarily effective, particularly the lead-in to the calligraphs.

O ye of little faith....

Once again, Griffin is filled with doubts—and is acutely aware of the ravages of illness and age:

> September 24, 1970
> Thursday
>
> Again, I note I have said earlier in this entry, that I "light up very slowly" (after sleep); when I should correctly say "gradually," because slowly implies the very concept of time that is largely evaporated in solitude.

In all of this I sense a perceptible diminution of intellectual gifts. I have noticed it for some time. I do not make any great thing of it. It does not concern me, except it is there and apparent. I am like a man who could once play the clavichord, and whose fingers have now lost their agility, and who hits all kinds of clinkers. What is it? Age? The shock of the illness? I do not know. The above messing up of language is a small example. There are many others. Certainly my vocabulary is reduced. In another sense, which is not bad, the sense of overwhelming mysteriousness grows in me, something that in my earlier years I would reduce to "understanding" ... to concepts, to synthesis. This facility is almost gone. I am deeply aware of it because I have such frequent contact with such gifted me in whose presence I tend to become almost mute insofar as intellectual speculation is concerned. The things that fill me now cannot be uttered with any accuracy, though I sometimes struggle to utter them. I find I end up writing about concrete (awful word) rather than speculative things —about the way the wind stirs the leaves of a single branch of a tree. I go along with it. I can do nothing else, and I am not at all sure this is not simply right for me at this time in my life.

These days in the hermitage were idyllic for Griffin, but he had not lost track of activism in the outside world:

January 13, 1971
Wednesday

Have heard that Phil Berrigan and five other men (four of them priests) and one nun have been indicted by a Federal Grand Jury on charges of plotting to kidnap Kissinger and also to blow up the heating systems of federal buildings. Phil is in prison, but the other six are all in custody. Dan and some others were not indicted, but were named as conspirators. What gives? Could this be possible, or is it some kind of monstrous mistake or monstrous suppression? It is a follow-up of J. Edgar Hoover's charges or allegations made public some time ago.

Griffin cannot escape *Black Like Me*, even in Gethsemani. He has a visit from "Brother Ambrose," who was, in Griffin's words, the "Mexican from the slums of Fort Worth":

March 25, 1971

It was one of the most moving hours I have spent in a long time. He did not really come her to talk about monastic life or anything else, really, but to tell me how much he thought of the book *Black Like Me*, and of his profound identification with it. We talked with a great union of spirit about his life and his family. He has a mother and two sisters still living in Fort Worth. I will go see them. His older sister recently lost her husband, who had been paralyzed for three years. The whole family is very poor. He had heard me speak in chapel Sunday and had decided that if we needed help with the housework or cooking, he would ask his sister to come help us. I suggested that there were times when we did desperately need help, and if she needed the work ...

Oh no ... he hadn't meant that. He had meant that it would be their way or repaying me for the stance I had taken. Dear God, I almost wept—the very poor contriving to help out someone in need.

July 3, 1971
Late afternoon.

Today is the anniversary of my being struck by lightning here. In spite of all the interruptions, this has been one of the happiest and most peace-filled and prayer-filled days I have ever known. The prayer of the heart goes on, no matter what I do. It is a conscious unconscious kind of self-perpetuating thing. Even when I awaken fitfully in the night that is the one thing I am first aware of—that the heart is praying incessantly as a counterpoint to whatever else goes on in me.

May 12, 1972. Griffin hears that Governor George Wallace had been shot. He writes in his journal:

Lord, I see and hear about me everywhere the insane rationalizations that we heard and saw surrounding Hitler in the thirties. The Germans were willing to leave the door open to unspeakable abuses against Jews and many non-Jews in order to support a man who promised to get rid of far more superficial abuses.

We are willing and eager to leave the door open to unspeakable abuses (including the war in Southeast Asia, the perpetuation of overt racism, the destruction of help to the poor) in order to avoid busing. What else really does it amount to? They can deny it until they are blue, but the great undertide of Wallacism is a manifestation of racism and nothing more.

Griffin's protracted stays at Gethsemeni end in September, 1972. His last journal entry reads:

I feel a profound sense of void when I think that my research in the hermitage at Gethsemani is now finished. Certainly that experience over the past few years has been one of the high points of my life. I am sad it is over, but forever grateful to have had it.

The years of the 1960s were Griffin's most productive and most turbulent. The *sturm und drang* following the publication of *Black Like Me* in 1961, the wide acclaim and the occasional outrages, the constant requests for speeches, appearances and travel lasted throughout the decade. His retreats into the Trappist world of Thomas Merton, from August 1969 to June, 1972, were spiritually renewing; he felt best when he was cloistered.

They may have been the most soul-satisfying episodes of his life.

Twelve |

The Merton Years:
Follow the Ecstasy

"I am known as a monk in love with a woman."

1972-1980
Texas and Gethsemani Abbey,
Kentucky

BOTH THE HERMITAGE JOURNALS and *Follow the Ecstasy: The Hermitage Years of Thomas Merton* were published posthumously, in 1981 and in 1983, respectively. Griffin was the first writer to use Merton's journals as a basis for a biography. Griffin viewed Merton's journals as a key to understanding Merton. In a later, more comprehensive biography, *The Seven Mountains of Thomas Merton*, Michael Mott apparently choose not to view Merton's journals in similar perspective.

Thomas Merton entered the Gethsemani Abbey in December, 1941 and remained there for twenty-seven years, until his death in Bangkok, in 1968.

Griffin's *Follow The Ecstasy* covers only four years, 1965, 1966, 1967 and 1968. Griffin didn't begin with Merton's first year in the abbey, or even his previous life in France and at Columbia University before he converted to Catholicism; Griffin wanted to write first about Merton's Gethsemani years because they were more immediate; Merton's journals and writings were there and other monks who knew Merton were still at Gethsemani.

In the section for April, 1965, Griffin writes about Merton, but the passage could have as easily referred to Griffin himself:

> "I am a Christian and a member of a Christian community. My brothers and I are to put aside everything else and recognize that we belong not to ourselves but to God in Christ. That we have vowed obedience that is intended to unite us to Christ, obedient, unto death, even the death on the cross." He meditated on obedience. Insofar as they truly desired God's will in them, then even the smallest and most ordinary things were made holy and great, and their lives were transformed. He regretted that so much of monastic obedience had become formal and trivial, and felt that renewal must mean above all a recovery of the sense of obedience to God in all things, and not just "obedience to rules and superiors where demanded, and then after that go wool-gathering where you may."

For those who did not know the back story of Griffin's ultimate inability to complete the book, *Follow the Ecstasy* may seem remarkably flat; it clearly reads like a first draft, left to be polished later. Griffin captures much more of the life of solitude, prayer and introspection at Gethsamine in *The Hermitage Journals* then he does in *Follow the Ecstasy*. In *Follow the Ecstasy* Griffin often refers to Merton as "the monk" or "Father Louis," the name Merton was given when he entered the cloister, or "the hermit," but those usages seem only to distance Griffin—and the reader—from Merton.

Typical of this usage is a section, from July, 1965:

> There followed days of great peace for the monk. He remarked that almost any day he could write "great peace" but this was a special and new dimension of peace—a tranquility that could not be attained by cultivation but was "given"'
>
> "One will, one command, one gift. A new creation of heavenly simplicity." However, this must be silent, secret, not for secrecy but because words would only falsify it.
>
> An oppressive heat, the first of that summer, settled over the area. On July 24 the monk was too torpid to pray seriously, but he kept trying. He made orangeade for supper and put in the freezer, thereby accidentally discovering how to make sherbet. He slept through the storms that came that night.

The entry for Merton in January 1966, shows Griffin at his stylistically best, even if, and especially *if*, this was a first draft:

> The snow continued heavy for two days, a blessing for the hermit for it helped guarantee

his solitude. No one would attempt to approach the hermitage in such weather. The illusion of time, of clocks and hours, dropped away. This freedom, with its accumulation of silent and solitude, elevated all aspects of his existence to the level of felicity. All activities fused in the miracle and he could no longer make any distinction between what are called the lower and higher elements of human living. His work, study, prayer and meditation flowed into acts needed to sustain his hermit life in the forest; to keep the fire going in the hearth; to sweep bits of straw and kindling used to start the fire; to pour a glass of drinking water and warm it by the fireplace for brushing his teeth; to pure stale bread crumbs on the porch and then watch the gathering of cardinals, mocking-birds, titmice, myrtle warblers and the small white-footed mice with their brown fur and big ears that scurried from the woodpile; to break ice in the rain barrel so the birds could drink, and draw from it a bucket of water to wash his coffee pot and dishes; to retrieve from the bare-ness of his kitchen shelf the large mason jar he used for his "night vessel" when the weather was too cold to go outside, and place it on the cement floor under his cot. In that climate of in-terior freedom each act was filled with joy and thanksgiving.

Griffin also writes segments like this about Merton:

Merton reflected on the moment of great loneliness he knew in his solitude but these were followed by other deeper moments of hope and understanding, as this morning, which

would not be possible in their purity anywhere
but in solitude.

Since there is no reference to Merton's journals
in this passage, Griffin presumably assumed he knew
Merton's psyche to this extent and could recreate
Merton's thoughts.

The year 1966 brought Griffin a problem in *Follow
The Ecstasy* which he may not fully anticipated, or may
not have been fully prepared to deal with.

Merton had entered a local hospital for hip surgery.
One of the nurses was Margie Smith: she entered his
room, and announced that she had been assigned to
him. She knew who Merton was—not only knew who he
was, but she herself had been in a convent. When she
left the room, Merton, the hermit, the monk often in
solitude, was unhappy when she was gone.

Griffin writes:

> From that first encounter, Merton, who had
> before sought to avoid attention, now devised
> pretexts to have Miss Smith return, and pro-
> longed the visits as much as possible. She also
> invented pretexts, bringing him extra sand-
> wiches or reading materials whenever she had
> a free moment.
>
> They talked hungrily and incessantly.
> Merton lent her his manuscript preface to the
> Japanese edition of *Thoughts in Solitude* in an
> effort to help her understand his hermit voca-
> tion. He believed her to be a solitary who fought
> solitude, feared it and rejected it. They had run
> into each other as questions. He hoped his pref-
> ace might help her by providing some answers.

Too, they were united in one painful common aspect of their experience: a loss of illusions about the character of religious organizations at the level of power manipulation and pure human emotion.

Then she disappeared; Merton discovered she was ill. He waited and waited—and even hobbled out toward the nurses' quarters, but did not see her.

Then she returned: "The room was filled with the light of freedom and joy," Merton wrote. "Pure joy. So pure one never even thought of it as joy." Merton had met her March 30; he had fallen in love quickly and she with him. During April, at Gethsemani, he wrestled with the problem of human love in the context of his existence as a Trappist monk.

In May, he again ventured out of Gethsemani and met her; they journeyed to Louisville where they met Merton's publisher James Laughlin of New Directions and Chilean poet Nicanor Parra.

Griffin writes:

> After supper Merton and Margie went off alone, walking aimlessly and talking. They found a couple of trailers parked in a field near the airport buildings and sat in the grass behind them to watch the sunset.

And, Griffin continues:

> They remained alone only a short time, perhaps half an hour, before rejoining James Laughlin and Nicanor Parra to drive back to the hospital.

It was Griffin's subtle implication that Merton and Margie Smith may have been intimate.

By June, word had spread in Gethsameni about him and *her*. Merton had to admit to himself: "I am known as a monk in love with a woman."

Ultimately, their relationship was impossible to sustain. At the end of June, he saw her for the last time. On July 12, Merton wrote, "I realized that no matter how much I may love Margie and be attached to her, there has never for a moment really been any choice."

Once, during this period, on a visit to his doctor in Louisville, Merton was "torn by loneliness and longing to talk to her" and was almost "visibly crying."

Merton made the final step back toward his life of solitude. On Thursday September 8, he read a short speech he had written:

> I, brother M. Louis Merton, solemnly professed monk of the Abbey of Our Lady of Gethsemani, having completed a year of trial in the solitary life hereby make my commitment to spend the rest of my life in solitude in so far as my health may permit.
>
> Made in the presence of Rt. Rev. Dom M. James Fox, Abbot of Gethsemani, September 8, 1966.

Merton saw Margie Smith twice again when he had to return the Lousiville hospital, but only briefly each time. She eventually moved away and married someone else.

The psychological distance that Griffin had shown with his use of "the monk"' or "Father Louis" or "the hermit" largely disappeared in Griffin's passages about Merton's love affair with Margie Smith. Here Griffin is at his most sympathetic; his narrative is more humane, caring. Griffin may well have thought of his own years of blindness and the joy of recovering his sight and seeing his wife and his two children for the first time. Griffin clearly sees Merton as troubled by his love for Margie Smith and his inability to be anything more that what he was: a Trappist monk, committed to solitude. These are the best, most evocative pages of *Follow the Ecstasy*.

The concluding section from mid-1966, the end of Merton's affair with Margie Smith, to 1968, seems largely anti-climactic. Griffin writes of the minutiae of Merton's daily life. Griffin's *The Hermitage Journals* is a more nuanced book; *Follow the Ecstasy*, can, however still be read as a supplement to Merton's major works and the four years that Griffin covers.

In an Epilogue, Griffin writes about Merton's beliefs; in this passage, Griffin seems clearly to be echoing his own philosophy as well:

> Having lived through the days of Nazi oppression, having seen racism at close hand in this country, having witnessed the establishment's suppression and character-assassination of those opposing United States involvement in the Vietnam war, and having worked with those struggling for human rights and peace, Thomas Merton realized that ethics based on consensus and expediency, rather than on principle, produced societies of a

monolithic mediocrity that always sought to destroy what they could not encompass.

The decision to face reprisals for the good of those who would persecute him had to be a person's own. Merton would not make such decisions for others, nor would be judge those who simply could not make those sacrifices; he commiserated deeply with those who attempted the sacrifice and caved in when reprisals were brought against them.

Thirteen |

A Chronicle of a Death Foretold

... with the patience of a twentieth-century Job ...

1970s
Fort Worth, Texas

JOHN HOWARD GRIFFIN WAS beset with more illness than any ten people deserved. In his last sojourn to France, before he became completely blind, he suffered malaria, probably contracted in the South Pacific.

Then the ten years of blindness. Griffin never raged against God for his handicap; he raged at himself momentarily, when he was at first unable to eat a meal without knocking over a wine glass or spilling his food. He never *ever* raged at God; by all accounts he considered it an act of Divine Will; God's place for him in the universe.

Then foot tumors, a condition he said he inherited from his father. And spinal malaria, which kept him paralyzed for a year, when he was completing *Nuni*.

And diabetes, which had been kept in check during the months he spent at Gethsemani, working on his Merton project, which eventually became *The Hermitage Journals* and *Follow the Ecstasy*.

But after he returned to Texas, his diabetes led to osteomyelitis, an inflammation and eventual deterioration of the bone marrow (of the lower spine).

The savage beating by the Klu Klux Klan in 1975 perhaps led to permanent kidney damage.

He lost part of one jaw and he had lung congestion.

High blood pressure. Heart disease.

Griffin faced all these illness with the patience of a twentieth-century Job ...

He continued, as far as he could, unending lectures, public appearances, travel and his own writing. But more and more he was dependent on a wheelchair, which he had used at Gethsemani.

He had a series of heart attacks. In 1979, one leg had to be amputated because of his diabetes.

For years Griffin had corresponded with Cornelia and Irving Sussman, who had contributed articles and essays to: *The Catholic Youth Encyclopedia*; *The New Catholic Encyclopedia*; *The Bridge*; *The Critic*; *America*; *Saturday Review*; *Catholic World*; *Way* and *Franciscan Herald*.

Like Griffin and Merton, the Sussmans were converts to Catholicism and they had published an authorized biography of Merton, *Thomas Merton*, (Macmillan, 1976).

Griffin seemed fascinated, even fixated, by his own decline. In his latter years, He often wrote to the Sussmans; and often began his letters with: Beloveds.

In the title of the novel by Gabriel Garcia Marquez, his letters were a *chronicle of a death foretold*. He seemed clearly to understand his own slow decline. These are excerpts from his letters to Cornelia and Irving Sussman.

June 4, 1971
Loves,

In great haste to tell you that I am back home after a nightmare trip. As I was leaving Gethsemani last Saturday a small tumor appeared on the hip. I went on to Davenport, and from there to South Bend. The tumor grew like mad, two or three inches a day, like a snake under the skin, and down around the back of my leg until it began to cut the circulation. I was in misery at South Bend but we got the Maritain book laid out Monday night and Tuesday a.m. and then I took the flight to Chicago and home. At the airport in Chicago I started going into shock. They tried to get me to an ambulance to go to the hospital in Chicago but I begged them to let me come on to Dallas. They did, and were marvelous, wrapping me in blankets, feeding me hot milk, etc.

I got here at 3:30 and was in surgery by 5. The diabetes was completely out of control then, but all I could feel was relief and gratitude that I had made it home.

It is all right now. But I am obliged to "guard the bed" until we get the thing healed and the diabetes under control. So all I seem able to do is sleep a lot—there is no pain now, thank God. They are pouring the antibiotics to me (sic) every four hours around the clock.

November 22, 1971
Beloveds,

I have not been able to work. The blood sugar is very high, fever, pain. But today the tests showed it coming down a bit into a safer level, and the doctor thinks this will increase the circulation and lessen the pains. If it is not much better in two weeks, they will put me in the hospital and get it straightened up. Anyway, I have gotten a little respite. I thought they would put me in the hospital today.

Sunday, January 6, 1974
Beloveds,

I am not sure just when I wrote you. Have I written since Christmas? Yes, I think so. I have been sedated quite a lot after the loss of another piece of jaw, and have been working very hard in a kind of daze from all of that. Today has been the best day. I got up early and got into the work and it went well (am off sedation now) and there was such a joy to it, in the quiet and chill of the empty house, with only a fire back here in my studio, with plenty of coffee, and a sense that I was really into the work, really with it all the way. I don't suppose for a writer there is any greater happiness than that.

January 7, 1974
Beloveds,

I have been so bad about answering your great letters —which have been such lights in our lives. The foot went bad again, terribly painful, and that made sedation necessary, and sedation just turns me into a zombie. The thing is better now and I am off sedation, thank God.

It appears now that the staph infection has moved on and become osteomyelitis, which is not good but nothing as bad as it used to be. It can be contained from spreading. I will go for x-rays on Thursday to see if in fact it is osteomyelitis and how far the infection has gone.

April 16, 1975
Beloveds,

Although I am not working as well as I should— because of so many demands on my time—these are good and happy days for us. I do very well and am out of pain in the mornings, and then begin to fall to pieces in the afternoons and the pain is pretty intense by evening. We are getting a new wheel chair to see if that will not stave off the pain after I have been up for a while. After hearing others' troubles, I begin to realize that just being surrounded by loving children and family and friends is a surpassing blessing.

November 21, 1975
Beloveds,

I am in a kind of limbo between surgeries (on the mouth)—the first one day before yesterday, and the second supposed to be yesterday, but they postponed it and have put me on heavy antibiotics for a few days and will operate again on Monday at 10:30 a.m. I am able to be up, and to do some work, but don't have much sense because of the sedation and the inability to eat— only liquids and that not very easy. Well, I'll be fixed up Monday, and hope to be able to take some food by Thanksgiving.

And this, in handwriting:

Nov. 24, 1976
Beloveds,
I am confined to bed until Jan. 1, at last. I damaged the heart in Montreal, pushing my wheel chair too great a distance to catch a flight. The officials would not let the priest with me go beyond the security gate.

I am on treatment now and the heart will begin repairing itself they hope. Besides the medication, it is a matter of total bed rest.

Monday December 6, 1976
Beloveds,
Not much news. I lie here and witness the struggle of a damaged heart trying to supply the needs of the body—and it is actually a very touching thing to experience—as though I were watching another person, quite detached from me, laboring to keep me alive. It makes it easier to be still, to do without all of those things this body has learned to like—the tobacco, the coffee, the food (most of it). Well, now all I can sense is that the organs are grasping for their share of oxygenated blood, and the heart is doing its best, and I am filled with gratitude for all it does.

December 11, 1976
Beloveds,
I am right here in bed, and the electrocardigraph yesterday showed both healing and complications (the kidneys, the diabetes fluctuating because of the heart). He doubled the

digitalis, added potassium, gave a prescription for potassium, wisdom, total chastity (eve in the heart) and total bed rest plus starvation. He said only the potassium could be supplied by the pharmacy. I would have to supply the rest myself. But there has been some healing and I am to stay still until Jan 10th and not do any kind of activity, and the danger of a coronary is diminished now.

January 13, 1977 Thursday
Beloveds,

Some hasty notes. Long careful examination yesterday. The wound is healing slowly but the congestive heart failure it produced has left the heart permanently damaged, so I am going to have to learn to live a new way. Everything is working against everything else (diabetes, atherosclerosis, etc.) And now the immediate danger is high blood pressure, which increases the danger of stroke or heart attack, I have to be very cautious, must have stress and tension minimized. Dr. Kyger says I should go into hiding somewhere, but since I can't (I have to be watched constantly) then it is a matter of the gravest important to have everything tranquil around me. For the next thirty days he is restricting visitors to one a day, and to no more than 15 minutes a visit.

I do not feel like a dying man, but only one who is aware of the danger.

And, again, in handwriting ...

Sat. March 11, 1977
Beloveds,

I just got home last night after surviving an acute myocardial infarction, so must now keep nitroglycerine with me at all times. I was very lucky. It is usually fatal within the first minutes; if you can survive three hours, there is hope. It hit suddenly, after much general improvement. Scar tissue from the heart injury caused the blockage. The pacemaker is working fine.

I guess God wants me to realize my life or death is in his hands. I didn't really need this to make me realize that!

This kind of trauma blocks my memory.

April 28, 1977
Beloveds,

My heart disease has become chronic and degenerative, after 6 months; and high blood pressure has been added. The lesser problems of the osteo and the eye have simply been ignored in this kind of perpetual emergency situation with the heart. Do not be sad. It is one of the most fascinating things I have ever experienced, and I only wish I had the strength to write about it. Everything is being done. I will not go to the hospital until it is finally necessary. Everything is new. It is new to have to live on the edge of death, never knowing if I will be alive an hour from now. It has become that kind of situation. I can still get up and walk around the house these days. I can still come to the typewriter some days, though I am unable to do any work. I carry nitroglycerine always on my person, when the attacks come, I take it under my tongue. If I can survive from 5-9 minutes, then that means I am o.k. for a while. For a while they came daily. This week there have been only two, so things are working out a little better. I grow stronger, begin to feel some spark of life between the attacks, but am out for hours afterward.

All for now, blesseds. Do write me when you can. I love your letters. Do not worry about any of this. I just felt you should know. I can conceivably live on a long time—a few years anyway; but that is not likely. I am utterly resigned and at peace in this area. I neither dread it nor look forward to it. I leave it entirely there where it belongs—in God's hands.

I still feel an immense, all consuming capacity to love; and I am surrounded by love, carried by it. What else, really, is there? You are among the most loved.

The following may be one of Griffin's journal entries; he sent carbons of his journal entries to the Sussmans when he did not write letters. He refers to his wife by her nickname Piedy. Dr. Ross Kyger is his attending physican. Griffin didn't notice or didn't care to change the mis-numbered items. Material underlined appears to have been underlined in pencil.

Kyger report, May 11, 1977

1). Blood pressure has risen to stroke point, or very near it, increasing blood pressure medicine.

2). Lower parts of body not receiving sufficient supply of blood. This requires a different kind of walking, shorter distances with rests between, but much longer eventual distances each day. Have to watch all lesions, especially the osteo for fear of gangrene.

4). Despite heart attacks last week, the heartbeat remains stable. Reducing pacemaker from four to three a day.

5). Chemical inbalance again. Reducing diuretic, increasing potassium.

6). Continue digitalis as before.

7). As a precaution against dying of shock during heart attack, I am to carry needle and Iodocaine dosage, to be inserted directly into heart by me or anyone around, if three nitro's have not relieved the attack. (Fr. George has already disqualified himself. He said if it happened when only he were here, he would not be able to stick the needle into my heart, I told him I could do it without any difficulty, and so could Piedy, in case I was too deeply in shock to manage it myself. In such an extremity, I am sure almost anyone could.) Most deaths, he says, are not caused by the heart attack itself, but by the trauma of pain that sends you into deep shock and it is the shock that kills. This is a new treatment being adopted as the first emergency treatment in hospitals, and Kyger wants me to have it with me, because I could die without getting to the hospital. He dyed a spot on my chest to show where the needle should be inserted in such an event.

8). He performed minor surgery on the foot and removed a small tumor from the cervix, in his office, with local anaesthesia. It required only three stitches and was caught before it could grow into any kind of fistula. He sent it to pathology, but is sure it is perfectly all right, since I have had such tumors many times before and is the same kind.

8). He expressed satisfaction over everything but the legs and the blood pressure and imbalance. Went over the x-rays and showed me all the results of the electrocardiagram and blood testing. There is not a great deal more than can be done, considering all the complexities (the diabetes, the osteo) I am extremely uncomfortable tonight, but all right. Cannot take pain medication because of the heart. Wanted to make these notes while my memory is fresh, before going to bed. The diagnosis remains essentially the same, not much chance of it getting better, but we can live on with this, keep a close check on everything. He said he is not giving up on me and never will give up on me. He says my character is somewhat of a <u>handicap</u> <u>and said we could not do much about that: he</u> <u>says if I would stop trying to carry all the cares</u> <u>and burdens of the world on my shoulders, stop</u> <u>weeping</u> over everyone's problems, the blood <u>pressure problem would not be so acute.</u> He ordered me not to do anything or leave the house without calling him first. He ordered me to have Piedy simply refuse to let any disturbing people or phone calls through, and says I can watch only non-violent and non-stressful programs on the TV; an he would rather I did not even watch the news—just let someone else tell me what is happening.

The following is a journal entry and was sent to the Sussmans:

August 8, 1977

Difficult to write about these days. The medical examination and test Saturday were pretty terrible—the worst yet. The heartbeat is less regular than it ever has been. I just spend more and more time flat on my back. ... The nights are mostly sleepless or filled with nearly unbearable nightmares at the very edge of sleep, where I seem half-awake but cannot evade or escape them. Sometimes I just have to sit on the edge of my bed to get them to go away. Most of them are filled with the heartlessness and cruelty I have seen through so much of my life and vocation —all of that comes back to haunt and terrify me as it did in the old days: the nazi days, the civil rights days. These visions leave me with a suffocating sense of grief— a desperation so great I feel I must do anything to escape them.

I put this down not to complain but to keep a kind of record. My experience now is far away from the experience most people connect with life. I try to stay connected with life, but it seems more and more distant and unreal to me.

My character is the greatest difficulty. The only thing that really holds me is trying to live and understand this experience. I get interested only in writing about it, and then I over-work and have terrible problems with pain and congestion. There is so much reality to be discovered in this kind of mortal helplessness that few people experience until the very end of their lives, if then.

Now, I am experiencing it from the "inside" and probably what saves me from just going on and dying is this hidden fascination with the process. All that really functions in me now is my brain: the hands become more and more numb. Since that little stroke, I am not supposed to do may lifting with my left arm (as if I could anyway). The physical heart is rapidly reducing its ability to function. The symbolic heart is on the contrary growing, as are feelings—so much so that they leave me almost exhausted with their ardor. They are also the source of a deep frustration, because I can no longer do for people what the heart and feelings ache to do.

In this part of a letter to the Sussmans, material was also underlined in pencil.

> 9/30/77
> Beloveds,
> This has been a chancy ten days. Extremely severe attacks continue to weaken. Another placquette flaked off into the brain, this one giving me such hearing distortion that I can no longer even tell what music sounds like and can only bear the softest speaking voices. Everything else is so loud and harsh it drives me up the wall. I have changed typewriters, because the louder clacking of the other one made typing unbearable. But the vital organs continue to be given enough blood, so I will go on like this until friend heart simply wears itself out or an attack takes me. I am weakened beyond believing. I cannot write seriously. I cannot even dictate because of the lack of breath.

In this next journal entry, Griffin describes how it feels to have not just one, but two, heart attacks. He had written ability, then added (inability) in the right margin, in pencil.

This brief memoir is doubly remarkable: that he could have survived these experiences so close to death's door and secondly, in his weakened condition, that he could record such vivid recollections.

The reference to Tom, was to Father Tom McKillop, a priest from Toronto, Canada, was Griffin's "confessor" during Griffin's last few years and a friend since 1972. Father Tom wrote a book about his friendship with Griffin, *Friendship and Second Innocence: Two Souls in Conversation.* Father McKillop, who became Tommy to Griffin, sponsored many of Griffin's journeys to Canada in the mid-1970s and traveled many times to Fort Worth to visit.

Luiz was Luiz de Moura-Castro, Brazilian pianist, who lived across the street from the Griffin's in Fort Worth, Luiz was studying with the legendary pianist Lili Kraus, who was then teaching at Texas Christian University. His wife Bridget was also a pianist; they had three little girls who were playmates of Amanda Griffin, the youngest of four Griffin children.

Fri. 1/6/78

I wish I could describe accurately what went on in those attacks—the fading, the reality of pain and suffocation, the absolute certainly that I was dying, the loss of pulse and heartbeat and the ability (inability) to breathe even when the oxygen was pouring into me, the sadness and release of tears, the terrifying loss of ability to focus ... searching faces and eyes, sure that when I could no longer see the expression in people's eyes I was gone—that as long as I could see that, focus on it, I had some chance. In the one, when I was here alone with Tom, he kept pressing hard on the left ventricle of my heart with one hand, and guided my breathing with his hand on my abdomen, pressing and releasing, reminding me to breathe in rhythm to the pressure and release. From a great distance I would hear his calm voice saying "squeeze my arm, John" and that would bring me back to try to obey, to concentrate on doing something. When I could no longer see anything but a fuzzy image of his face, he lowered his head close so I could see his eyes—remind me to pray— anything to keep me attached to the real and bring me back from the distance. The sadness was replaced with a profound sense of gratitude as he seemed to bring me back by the sheer force of his efforts, his inventiveness.

The second attack was similar to the first. I was in my bed ... the family in another part of the house. I felt the first great pain and the congestion and all I could think was that this one was starting so heavily I had no chance. I got up and staggered into Tom's room where we had reserved the sacrament in order to give the Moura Castros and Piedy communion a little later. I felt a compulsion to be there with the reserved sacrament. Luiz and Piedy found me, already beyond the ability to focus or see much.

A period of darkness and detachment followed. Dimly I was aware of someone putting nitro under my tongue, a great pressure on my chest, people, Tom's voice telling me to breathe. I tried to obey. Vague surprise to find

I was under the oxygen mask. (I discovered later that someone had carried that heavy tank to the bedside in the other room.) Things came back. Tom's voice kept coming—the only voice I could hear. Then I heard Piedy's anxious breathing. She was standing over me, leaning all her weight forward to press the left side of the heart. Feeling of guilt to frighten her so. She put her head close to my face so I could see her. Tom's voice. Someone holding my left hand tightly to monitor the pulse (which simply stopped). Feeling of people and silence, people pouring all their life and energy into me. And then a completely new thing— a flooding sense of elation, the purest kind of joy seemed to spread through all my tissues, a kind of amuse-ment, to desire to laugh, the return to focus and astonishment that so many people were present around my bed. Piedy stood above me, Tom at her side seated on the bed, making me breathe with a kind of artificial respiration.

Luiz came and sat beside me where Piedy had stood. Somehow my oxygen mask had been removed. He looked down at me with an almost angelic expression on his face, bent for-ward and kissed me on the cheek. Violent head pains from the nitro, cold clothes on my head and neck ... but great happiness, because I had obviously died for a moment, having ceased to breathe and lost all pulse, and was saved by the artificial respiration and the oxygen. Again the flooding sense of gratitude. It is transforming how you love people who give you back the very breathe of life, who carry you through such a death—it is the purest, most intense essence of loving we felt in that room afterward; it is a profound intimacy you share from then on, because you can never feel the same afterward. Many times my glance caught Tom's. I cannot tell what he was thinking but I am sure I was transparent, thinking "that is how many times during this year that that blessed man has saved me from dying."

So, all in all, because of the blessings, this is a time of the most powerful richness and the most terrible wretchedness of my life. The fact that they happen to coincide is the greatest blessing of all. That prevents it from degenerating into Hemingway's version of a "dog's death." I can see how it would be that if something of great love did not penetrate the ultimate loneliness of the struggle.

Journal entry, Feb. 3, 1978:

Friday: Extreme killing pain the past 24 hours—almost maddening in the night, absorbing all other perceptions until the body is reduced to begging abjectly for some end to it, for some relief. The only escape, or rather diversion, from those burning pains comes in flashes of temptations to put an end to it. The thing gnaws at my entrails like a buzzard. Fishbones in the throat.

How foolish everything sounds, especially optimism, especially the facile utterances about God and love and sharing when these things seem to stop several miles short of death and turn aside to more comfortable climates. I have not lost my faith. I am just not sure the faith of most can come along with me into such harshness. I pray it can, because it is too lonely here in this darkness.

Another hate letter, this one from Wichita Falls. The main difference between these and the old ones is that these seem both more literate (few misspelled words) and more merciless, more deliberately and sadistically degrading. This one concludes: "You just keep sucking that black ass and maybe some day soon you will go into a diabetic coma. Maybe with a little luck you can have some nigger pallbearers.

"Signed with all the admiration due you
—A White Man"

2/23/78
Beloveds,

Your letter, Irv, which was waiting for me when I returned from the hospital yesterday, caused me pain in sensing your pain and bewilderment. One of my letters either did not get mailed or I intended to write it and did not. I thought you knew about the radiation, and in fact was mystified that you made nothing of it in your letters. The intestinal tumor began growing a couple of months ago, very rapidly, and we had to undertake a series of six treatments that leave the most paralyzing and devastating after-effects that just knock me out with pain day and night for three or four days. That's why I have not written as much as I ordinarily would. Yesterday's was, we hope, pray, plead, the last treatment. The mass has been reduced, but we cannot yet be sure it will stay that way. Here all the time I thought you knew and were praying for that!

Also, there is a continuing distant, detached kind of interest in "observing" what is happening to this human person, as though a part of me were not really involved in the more gruesome and humiliating aspect of it.

The following letter was written approximately June 6, 1978. Elisabeth Kübler-Ross (July 8, 1926– August 24, 2004) was a Swiss-born psychiatrist, a pioneer in near-death studies and the author of *On Death and Dying* (1969), where she first discussed what is now known as the Kübler-Ross model.

She was the recipient of twenty honorary doctoral degrees and by July, 1982 had taught, in her estimation 125,000 students in death and dying courses in colleges, seminaries, medical schools, hospitals and social-work institutions.

Beloveds,

I know you have been desperately worried, but I could not write you in the past ten days. May 25, in a great kind of lull between attacks and feeling I was dying inside, I took off and went to Toronto where I was met by Tom McKillop (I did this with Dr. K's permission here. He said I might as well try anything now. I was in consultation with five doctors there, all of whom confirmed that is nothing medically can be done, but I came back to life simply because when I am there, everything explodes around my bedside and I get happy and things start happening. My ten-day total was 13 attacks, nearly all of them monitored by the doctors, the establishment of a home for juvenile teen-age girls; the final establishment (with phone calls to Belgium) of a branch of the University of Peace in Toronto (Under Ft. Tom's direction); endless counseling with multiple handicapped, paraplegics, etc.;

1 outing to visit with prisoners; 1 brief public appearance to introduce Elisabeth Kübler-Ross; presence but not participation in one of the Sharon family week-ends (with 200 people there, though I stayed isolated); helping get a priest of remarkable achievements released from his present duties to collaborate with Ft. Tom. In other words in the midst of the deepest sickness I was functioning and gloriously happy. Dr. Kyger found me no worse physically for having done all this than I would have been lying here in bed. He said "Every one of my colleagues and every cardiac patient in the area would think we were both crazy for having taken this chance." I told him I felt that I had come back from a place of life where I somehow caught back onto at least the inner coming alive, and that I was going somehow to keep that. Piedy is delighted to see me so much happier. The atmosphere here is much less somber, although there is no chance I can fail to die soon. But at least I have hopes that I will remain active inside until the last. The situation was so physically bad in Toronto that they had to call Dr. Kyger to consult with him. Anyway, pray that I am able to sustain the great interior aliveness and not fall back into this terrible sense of helplessness, loneliness, and uselessness in just waiting for the end. I had a full day with Elisabeth K-Ross in which we did not talk about me, but about other people and quite particularly about her own problems. She is a

beautiful and saintly woman, utterly simple and devoid of all affectations. In so many ways, she reminded me of you, Cornelia.

Griffin again writes to Irving and Cornelia Sussman; the writer who took over Griffin's Merton biography was Michael Mott. His book *The Seven Mountains of Thomas Merton* was published by Houghton Mifflin in 1984. The Legacy Trust Griffin refers to was the Thomas Merton Legacy Trust, holders of the rights to Merton's work and manuscripts.

Monday, July 17, 1978

Beloveds,
Your wonderful letter arrived this moment. We have been concerned about the same thing, the Merton biography, on which I have worked for ten years now. This has been almost an unendurable burden over me in the last two years of growing helplessness, especially since I constantly receive pressuring mail about it. I will not be able to work anymore, and I have finally decided at the end of last week with Houghton Mifflin and the Legacy Trust that it is no longer reasonable for me to hold up this work. Another author has been found, apparently very fine. He will do the work, but wants to research from scratch, and I cannot but admire that. Perhaps someday my own work may appear, but I cannot think of that now, nor am I able to work with anyone else, as I had hoped. I have outlived the prognosis but that cannot last much longer—the degeneration of heart functions, arteries, etc. is steady and except for moments of

reprieve, cannot bear the continued responsibility for anything to do with a work so massive.

So, although all of my materials have been made available to the new biographer, the work is really out of my hands now, and I have no inclination to grieve over this. It is so transparently God's will. Even though it may seem an inexplicable waste in human terms, I am no longer able to feel it is ... nothing is lost as far as I am concerned except the satisfaction of having completed a work of my heart. I cannot even find it in my heart to feel any regret. I am confident that if it was not meant for me to do this work to the end, then it will be done by someone else. All I can feel right now is a great sense of relief that the matter is out of my hands, especially since I am too ill to even work with someone else.

I have taken care of my wife and children's near future, and now I am refusing to count the days or the weeks or months I have. I am refusing to think that soon I will die or that some medically inexplicable healing might occur.

Griffin's letters get shorter ...

Friday, Oct. 5, 1979

Beloveds,

A wonderful letter from you today when I returned from the bone specialist. He confirmed what I was pretty sure of—I will soon lose my left leg and they will have to amputate some from the stump of my right leg as well. I cannot use any artificial limbs. The family is very upset, even though everyone is acting alright. God knows what we will do—so many problems involved in having no legs as compared to having one. We'll˚know when the time comes, I suppose.

Great love to both of you from all of us.

His journal entries also become shorter....

October 14, 1979

Beginning tomorrow, the therapist will come three times a week in an attempt to build up my arm and shoulder muscles, but they are in poor shape and I don't see how they can be built up sufficiently at my age to do me any good. Anyway, I can handle the wheel chair, and with the one leg can get in and out with no help ... but how will that work without the leg? Will someone have to put me in and out of the chair? God, I hope not. Surely I am not going to become that totally helpless. There must be ways.

I do have the strength, new to me, to go up the ramp from the living room into this part of the house ... if I don't try it too often.

These paragraphs are written over a long period of time—a few lines, then bed rest, a few more lines, then medication. The legs feel as though they are broken in a half-dozen spots. The doctor says they are ready to come off, but the heart is not ready for the trauma of removing them yet.

Thursday, Oct. 18, 1979

Most of the day with doctors and nurses—
the pulse is very low. We will try another month
of anti-biotics for the legs, since the heart cannot stand surgery on any part of the body now.
Am dead tired and in pain despite the hypo.
Any way you look at it, the reports are dismal,
but at least I escape the surgery for a while.

Sunday, November 10, 1979

Deep sickness last evening and this
morning. Very cold, especially with so little
circulation.

November 12, 1979

To the doctor's yesterday. The vital signs
are so poor they can do no more surgery. Hard
attack last evening. another in the night. No
sleep until around 6 this morning. Very tired.
Father Tom called last night to find out
what the doctors said. He may get to come and
see me again, especially if I can live until Xmas.

Monday, Nov. 19, 1979

Very difficult to make these notes. I don't
really know why I make them. Something inside says "go back to bed'' or "take sedation." ...
"knock yourself out."

Friday, Nov. 23, 1979

Later—3 pm. Dozing in my chair, my mind
a codeined blank, drifting into memories that
have no time or place but are filled with the
people I love—a panorama without sequence
(my grandmother lifting me off the floor when
I could no yet walk ... now Tom lifting me off he
floor when I fall and can no longer walk, etc.)
Where are they now, these beloved ones—in
their graves or going about living their lives—
mostly for the good of others.

Sat. Dec 8, 1979

Unable to get up for three days, but around
noon today I felt stronger and am in my wheel
chair. Christmas is near and I have not been
able to do a thing about it.

Later, evening—sicker and sicker until the
pain was unbearable—as though all my bones
were broken.. My stump opened up—for no
apparent reason. A very long day. Talked late
in the evening, after taking codeine, with Dr.
Handa and with Tom. Tom said: "I was afraid
this would be a very rough day for you ... it's
a feast day." Only then did I realize it was the
feast of the Immaculate Conception.

I ran out of water, and the heat was very
high. I called and called for help but couldn't
awaken anyone and was too weak to get into my
wheel chair....

Sunday, Dec. 9, 1979

Too sick to write.

Thursday, Jan. 17, 1980

Nearly all of yesterday in bed with heart pains.

Stayed in bed until early this afternoon.

Today is the Feast of St. Anthony, with its marvelous antiphon "The man will flourish like the palm tree ..."

In the next journal entry, he clearly wanted to write *relapse* of the flu....

Monday, Jan 21, 1980

Piedy has had a release of the flu. It is cold and rainy outside. My mother is here taking care of both of us. My left foot is too painful to sleep, so I didn't. Everyone urges me to take the pain medication, but though it makes me sleep it turns me into a zombie during the waking hours and I tried to get off of it last night, so I am even more of a zombie today for not having slept.

Tuesday, Jan. 22, 1980

Little sleep. I now have seven ulcers on the foot and leg. Impossible to get into a position that allows for sleep.

Thursday, Feb. 28, 1980

I struggle to do a little work, but these are bad moments. It is very difficult to get out of bed. My leg aches from the hip down, and my mind is a blank of premonition of death. It is not something to give in to, but it becomes more and more difficult not to.

March 17, 1980

Days and nights of nearly unbearable suffering. I put down what I can. Despite myself, I feel a great closeness to those very old people still living and those dear to me who have died. Such thoughts simply are burned in my consciousness. No desire to eat or drink. I have to force myself. I usually read the mass because the texts speak so directly to me.

In late spring, 1980, Griffin no longer had the strength to continue his journal entries or write to his friends.

I have fought the good fight,
I have finished the race,
I have kept the faith ...

John Howard Griffin died September 9, 1980 of a cerebral hemorrhage. He was 60 years old.

Shortly after his death, Elizabeth was asked how he died.

Her explanation was simple: "He died ..." she said, "... of everything."

Epilogue

Before his death, some of John Howard Griffin's books became neglected: *The Devil Rides Outside*, *Nuni* and surely *The Church and the Black Man*. In this age of electronic books, they are appearing again as e-books to be read on devices like the Amazon Kindle.

The Devil Rides Outside is an anachronism; *Nuni* a curiosity. *The Hermitage Journals* and *Follow the Ecstasy* should be considered supplemental titles to the Merton canon.

But, since 1961, throughout much of the world, John Howard Griffin's enduring legacy can be writ large in three words:

black like me

Notes on Sources

Chronology

Page

vii   Griffin was born Howard Griffin. He later added John as a pen-name, Robert Bonazzi, Man in the Mirror, pp. 5.

viii   Elizabeth Ann (Piedy) Holland ... her parents nicknamed her "Pie" because supposedly that was her first word. Griffin named her Piedy; she apparently never liked either nickname, Robert Bonazzi, e-mail to author, June 10, 2010. A caveat to the reader ... viii"3,000 single-spaced pages ..." Bonazzi, Man in the Mirror, pp. 170.

A caveat to the reader ...

xiii   "3,000 single-spaced pages ..." Bonazzi, *Man in the Mirror*, pp. 170. Columbia University's Rare Book and Manuscript Library is the main repository of Griffin material; Columbia has 37 boxes of Griffin manuscripts, letters, essays and other material from his life.

Prologue

Page

xvii   One of his favorite words was strange ..., *Scattered Shadows: A Memoir of Blindness and Vision*, (Maryknoll, N.Y., Orbis Books, 2004), pp. 227.

Chapter 1

Page

1   His mother Lena had studied ... Robert Bonazzi, Introduction, in *Scattered Shadows*, pp. 12.

2   "My father was a man ..." Studs Terkel. *American Dreams: Lost and Found.* (New York: Pantheon Books, 1980), pp. 282.

3   He became an assistant to Dr. Pierre Fromenty. Bonazzi, in *Scattered Shadows*, pp. 13.

3   Co-authored ... Intrepretation of the Ornaments ... *Ibid.,* pp. 71.

3   At 19, Griffin was a member of the French Underground ... Robert Bonazzi, e-mail to author, March 14, 2010.

3   "I had worked in France ..." *Scattered Shadows*, pp. 282-283.

4   When one of his student friends ... and This counter with anti-Semitism ... Griffin archives Columbia University.

5   Having witnessed the tragic effects of the Holocaust ... Bonazzi, in *Scattered Shadows*, pp. 13.

5   Returned to France ... Robert Bonazzi, e-mail to author, Mar. 14, 2010.

5   Nadia Boulanger ... www.wikipedia.org.

6   Beethoven's Opus 131 Quartet ... Griffin archives, Columbia University.

7   "A staggering novel ..." back dust jacket copy, hardcover edition, *The Devil Rides Outside*, Smiths, Inc., 1952.

8   Griffin's real mentor ..., Bonazzi, in *Scattered Shadows*, 11.

8   Hussar later returned ..., *Man in the Mirror*, pp. 12.

8   "We talk of my trip ..." *The Devil Rides Outside*, pp. 24.

9   "What is it, Jacques? ..." *Ibid.*, pp. 32.

9   "A gasp from the child ...." *Ibid.*, pp. 39.

10   "Monastic formality gives way ..." *Ibid.*, pp. 60.

11   "There Father ..." *Ibid.*, pp. 62-63.

12   "My God, my God ..." .bid. pp. 112-113.

13   "My sigh ..." *Ibid.*, pp. 590. 13

     "the novel wrote me into the church ..." and "Griffin was baptized ..." *Scattered Shadows*, pp. 11.

Chapter 2

Page

14   "Assigned to study ..." Bonazzi, *Scattered Shadows*, pp. 13.

15   Floridan Dialect chart, John Howard Griffin archives, Columbia University.

15   "While living with Pacific islanders ..." Robert Bonazzi, "Afterword," *Black Like Me*, The Definitive Griffin estate Edition, Wings Press, 2006, pp. 219-220.

16   Married a south Pacific Island woman, Robert Bonazzi, e-mail to author, June 7, 2010.

16   The title page of *The Devil Rides Outside* shows the publisher as Smiths, Inc. In *Nuni*, Houghton Mifflin lists the same firm as Smith's Inc.

17   "while the first novel ..." Bonazzi, *Scattered Shadows*, pp. 11.

17   John Howard is ... *Ibid.*, pp. 11.

17   "Do you want a name?" Griffin, *Nuni*, pp. 165-166.

18   "hearing, smelling, tastings and touching," Bonazzi, *Scattered Shadows*, pp. 11.

19   *The Dallas Morning News* ... Sunday, May 20, 1956.

23   "By 1945 ..." *Scattered Shadows*, pp. 21.

25   "Then the high, uneven ...." *Ibid.*, pp. 32-33.

Chapter 3

Page

28   "I was stupefied ..." *Ibid.*, pp. 36.

28   "We continued ..." *Ibid.*, pp. 36.

29   "I feared myself ..." *Ibid.*, pp. 41.

30   "I soon perceived ..." *Ibid.*, pp. 52.

31   "You didn't come for a book ..." *Ibid.*, pp. 61.

32   "like candlelight seen through dense fog." *Ibid.*, pp. 99.

32   "I knew that those ..." *Ibid.*, pp. 98.

33   "I forced the words out ..." *Ibid.*, 98-99.

33   "When I tried to eat ..." *Ibid.*, pp. 100.

34   "Learn to reach ..." *Ibid.*, pp. 100.

34   How would he urinate ...? *Ibid.*, pp. 102.

34   The old monk snapped his fingers .... *Ibid.*, pp. 101.

34   "There are two main activities.." *Ibid.*, 107-108.

35   "paralysis of caution." *Ibid.*, pp. 114.

35   "I fell into gullies ..." *Ibid.*, pp. 116.

36   "To most sighted people ..." *Ibid.*, pp. 119.

36   "learned all the Brailles," Terkel, *American Dreams: Lost and Found*, pp. 284.

36   "I felt no loss of dignity, *Scattered Shadows*, pp. 123.

37   "If he used a deck of Braille cards ..." *Ibid.*, pp. 122.

38   "She opened up a new world for me," *Ibid.*, pp. 129.

38   Griffin was born Howard Griffin, but took the pen-name John Howard Griffin after the publication of *Black Like Me*, as there was a British poet, Howard Griffin. Friends and family called him Howard, Robert Bonazzi to author, June 6, 2010.

39   ... learned to type ..., *Scattered Shadows*, pp. 131.

39   "Then the characters ..." *Ibid.*, pp. 132.

40   "Each time I came ..." *Ibid.*, pp. 132.

40   "In my first attempt at a novel ..." *Ibid.*, pp. 133.

40   ... first person narrative ..., *Ibid.*, pp. 133.

40   "Handbook for Darkness," *Ibid.*, pp. 133-134.

41   "A private journal ..." *Ibid.*, pp. 135.

42   *Working Days: The Journal of The Grapes of Wrath* was published by The Viking Press, New York, 1989; *Journal of a Novel: The East of Eden Letters* was published by The Viking Press, New York, 1969.

43   Robert Bonazzi says five ..., e-mail to author, May 3, 2010.

44   A second printing ... *Scattered Shadows*, pp. 155.

44   "I had always been ...," *Ibid.*, pp. 160.

45   "The ramifications of such a statue ..." *Ibid.*, pp. 179.Associated Press article, in Griffin archives, Columbia University.

46   The landmark ruling ..., biographical summary, Griffin archives, Columbia University.

46 And Frankfurter wrote, "it is clear ....," *Scattered Shadows*, pp. 224.

47 A magnificent statement, *Ibid.*, pp. 224.

47 "What Happened in Mansfield," monograph, Griffin Archives, Columbia University.

48 "I had been very close to Nuni ...," *Ibid.*, pp. 194-195.

48 The tribal islanders were ..., Robert Bozanni, e-mail to author, May 3, 2010.

48 "Now it is gone ...," *Scattered Shadows*, pp. 196.

Chapter 4

Page

49 *Darkness Visible* is the title of a 1979 novel by William Golding and also the title of novelist William Styron's memoir of descent into, and recovery from, depression so deep it almost killed him. (New York: Random House, 1990).

49 "Redness swirled ...," *Scattered Shadows*, pp. 213.

50 "I sat in the chair ...," *Ibid.*, pp. 213.

51 "He gave me a shot ...," *Ibid.*, pp. 214.

51 "My wife and children ...," *Ibid.*, pp. 214-215.

51 "I prayed vaguely ...," *Ibid.*, pp. 215.

52 "I couldn't control the vision ...," *Ibid.*, 215.

52 "There were reporters and photographers ..." *Ibid.*, pp. 216.

53 "The next morning ...," *Ibid.*, pp. 216.

53   Lyndon Johnson quotation, *Ibid.*, pp. 215-217.

54   Newspaper headlines filed in the Griffin archives at Columbia University were clipped exactly the wrong way; names of the newspapers were omitted, but they were Dallas-Fort Worth newspapers.

54   "Second Sight," *Time*, January 21, 1957, pp. 60.

55   "Finally, the doctors ...," *Scattered Shadows*, pp. 217.

55   "Many people wondered ...," *Ibid.*, pp. 217.

56   "The probable cause ...," Griffin, *Available Light: Exile in Mexico*, pp. 115.

56   "March 12, 1957 ...," *Scattered Shadows*, pp. 225.

57   He got $10,000 .... Robert Bonazzi to author, June 7, 2010.

57   "I asked Mr. Butler ...," *Land of the High Sky*, pp. v-vii.

59   J. Frank Dobie and Walter Prescott Webb were historians of the west. Dobie spent years on the faculty of the University of Texas.

60   Griffin's "first draft exceeded 1,300 pages ...," *Land of the High Sky*, pp. x.

Chapter 5

Page

61   Ray Sprigle's name ..., *In the Land of Jim Crow*. New York: Simon and Schuster, 1949, pp. 216. The Headliners' Club is an Austin, Texas-based journalism awards organization.

62   Attended Ohio State University for one year and left .... another non-graduate of Ohio State University was James Thurber who could never pass Botany classes because he could not see into a microscope. Ohio State never gave him a waiver for that class because of his bad eyesight; eventually Thurber left without graduating.

62   "newspaper vagabond ..." two others who did the same thing were Mark Twain and Harold Ross, who eventually was founding editor of *The New Yorker.*

62   I Was a Negro in the South for Thirty Days ..., Armistead S. Pride and Clint C. Wilson II. *A History of the Black Press*. Washington, D.C.: Howard University Press, 1997, pp. 135.

62   "... and in more than six months ...," *In the Land of Jim Crow*, pp. 19.

63   "I became ...," *Ibid.*, pp. 7.

63   "Mr. Sprigle's report ...." *Ibid.*, pp. vii-viii.

64   "There are only two possible solutions ..." *Ibid.*, pp. vii-viii and "You begin to get a better idea ..." *Ibid.*, pp. 31-32

66   "She is worn and aged ...,' *Ibid.*, pp. 43-44.

66   "So this is what ...'" *Ibid.*, pp. 50-51.

68   Chapter titles, *Ibid.*, pp. v.

68 Chapter titles, *Black Like Me,* pp. 3-10. All page references to *Black Like Me* are from the Definitive Griffin Estate Edition, second Wings Press edition with index, San Antonio, 2006.

69 The Mason-Dixon line runs across the southern state line of Pennsylvania and down the east-west borderline of Maryland and Delaware, with Pennsylvania and Delaware in the north, Maryland in the south. It is, or was, generally considered the dividing line between the north, with its sensibilities and culture, and the old south (prior to the 1960s), with its own sensibilities and culture.

69 "For years the idea haunted me ...," and "How else except ...," *Black Like Me,* pp. 3.

70 Shaved their heads: *In the Land of Jim Crow,* pp. 21; *Black Like Me,* pp. 11.

70 "We'd roll along ...," *In the Land of Jim Crow,* pp. 6.

71 "He punched his hat back ...," and "He made a huge sign of the cross ...," *Black Like Me,* pp. 56.

72 Griffin never knew ..., Robert Bonazzi, e-mail to author.

72 "The title meant nothing to me ...," Grace Halsell, *Soul Sister,* Fawcett Crest paperback edition, pp. 15. (All quotations from are from the Fawcett Crest edition.)

73 "The seed is planted ...," *Ibid.,* pp. 16.

73 "He read it quietly ...," *Ibid.,* pp. 22.

74 "One can kill a person ...," *Ibid.,* pp. 23.

74 "After I take the medication ..." *Ibid.,* pp. 33.

74 "She got contact lenses ...," *Ibid.,* pp. 40.

74 "What about the medication ...," *Ibid.,* pp. 44.

75   "In two or three weeks ...," *Ibid.*, pp. 44.

75   "a walnut stain ...," *Ibid.*, pp. 45.

75   "At the bank ...," *Ibid.*, pp. 49.

75   "Yes, I've packed ...," *Ibid.*, pp. 60.

76   "I kept walking ...," *Ibid.*, pp. 63.

76   "It's not that people ...," *Ibid.*, pp. 63-64.

76   "I study the faces ...,' *Ibid.*, pp. 75.

77   "Hey! Stupid ...," *Ibid.*, pp. 88.

77   "Harlem in some ways ...," *Ibid.*, pp. 130.

77   "With three or four exceptions ...," *Ibid.*, pp. 140.

78   "You will go there and get yourself killed ...," *Ibid.*, pp. 219.

Chapter 6

Page

79   "The real story ...," *Man in the Mirror*, pp. 171.

80   "... black people never asked him ...," *Ibid.*, pp. 1.

81   "... suddenly mysterious and frightening ...," *Black Like Me*, pp. 3.

82   "The chemical was Oxsoralen ...," Bonazzi, in *Man in the Mirror*, pp. 37 and in www.wikipedia.org. An urban myth has circulated that Oxsoralen poisoned Griffin's system and led to his death, but Griffin had a wide variety ailments throughout his life, including diabetes and a series of heart attacks in his later years. The urban myth is, apparently inaccurate in Griffin's case, but Michael Jackson used Oxsoralen to treat vitiligo to darken major white spots on his body, for some time prior to his death.

82   "... up to 15 hours a day ...," *Man in the Mirror,* pp. 37.

82   Living in a slave cabin ...,*Ibid.,* pp. 41.

83   "Now you go into oblivion ...," *Black Like Me,* pp. 11, and *Man in the Mirror,* pp. 41.

83   "Turning off the lights ...," *Black Like Me,* pp. 11-12.

85   "This seminal passage ...'" *Man in the Mirror,* pp. 43-44.

Chapter 7

Page

86   ... in the slave cabin of the Levys ..., *Man in the Mirror,* pp. 41. "I was a man born old ..." *Black Like Me,* pp. 13.

87   "Through a crude but mysterious ...," *Man in the Mirror,* pp. 44."Within less than two hours ...," *Man in the Mirror,* pp. 45.Selections from "The Intrinsic Other," in *Man in the Mirror,* pp. 47. In that essay Griffin uses the word endredged. He probably meant endrudged, which means to enslave. This could be a simple misprint or a mistake of translation. Griffin originally wrote that essay in French, to be published in a magazine in Belgium.

87   "Almost the deepest shock ...," Griffin, in Bonazzi, *Man in the Mirror,* pp. 47.

88   "Come all this way ...," Griffin, in Bonazzi, *Man in the Mirror,* pp. 47.

89   "What are you looking at me ...," *Black Like Me,* pp. 22.

89   "... sat sphinx-like ..." and "I learned a strange thing ..." *Ibid.*, pp. 22.

89   "Is there something familiar ...," *Black Like Me*, pp. 24 and *Man in the Mirror*, pp. 51.

90   "Because Williams had mastered ....," *Man in the Mirror*, pp. 51.

90   "Most of these people had taught me ...," Griffin, in *Man in the Mirror*, pp. 51.

91   "Way too well dressed for a shine boy ...," *Black Like Me*, pp. 24.

91   "The illusion of ...," *Ibid.*, pp. 26.

91   "When they want to sin ...," *Ibid.*, pp. 28.

91   A black woman in a white dress ..., *Ibid.*, pp. 26.

92   "My feeling of disorientation ...," *Ibid.*, 33.

92   "On Chartres Street ...," *Ibid.*, pp. 43-44.

92   Griffin walked through the streets ..., *Ibid.*, 35-38.

93   "The word 'nigger' ...," *Ibid.*, pp. 38.

93   "answered rudely and ...," *Ibid.*, pp. 51

94   "Once again a 'hate stare' ...," *Ibid.*, pp. 52.

94   "It is by justice ..." and "He who is less than ..." *Ibid.*, pp. 53.

94   The Christophe episodes appear in *Black Like Me*, pp. 54-59 and in *Man in the Mirror*, pp. 69-73.

95   "He allowed the whites to get off ...," in *Black Like Me*, pp. 61-62 and in *Man in the Mirror*, pp. 73-74.

95   "Given the name of a contact ...," *Ibid.*, pp. 66-67 and in *Man in the Mirror*, pp. 76-77.

96   "Nigger, what are you ..." *Black Like Me*, pp. 67 and *Man in the Mirror*, pp. 76; "negatives were blank," *Black Like Me*, pp. 68 and *Man in the Mirror*, pp. 77.

96   "Hattiesburg, November 14 ...," *Black Like Me*, pp. 69 and *Man in the Mirror*, pp. 78-79.

96   "I felt disaster.," *Black Like Me*, pp. 71 and *Man in the Mirror*, pp. 80.

97   Martin Luther King Jr. and James Baldwin, www.wikipedi.org profiles.

97   "Watts riots ...," and "Rodney King riots ...," www.wikipedia.org entries.

98   "Where you from?" *Black Like Me*, pp. 104-105.

99   "He spoke in a tone ...," *Ibid.*, pp. 105.

99   The black man, his wife and six children ..., *Ibid.*, pp. 108-118.

100   "After breakfast of coffee ...," *Ibid.*, pp. 117.

100   "for all the children ..." *Man in the Mirror*, pp. 102.

100   John Steinbeck's *The Grapes of Wrath*. New York: The Viking Press, 1939.

101   "Here, the Negro has ...'" *Black Like Me*, pp. 121.

102   It was "nerve-wracking ...," *Ibid.*, pp. 123.

102   "I was once more ...," *Ibid.*, pp. 124.

102   "I developed a technique ...," *Ibid.*, pp. 126.

103   "One former Georgia Governor Griffin ...," *Ibid.*, pp. 133.

Chapter 8

Page

104 *Obscene in the Extreme* was the title of a book by Rick Wartzman about how Steinbeck's book was banned in small towns in California. New York: Public Affairs Press, 2008.

105 "Let me tell you a story ...," in Thomas Fensch, *Steinbeck and Covici: The Story of a Friendship,* pp. 21.

106 "I realize the hatred ...," *Man in the Mirror,* , pp. 125.

107 "... began receiving death threats ...," *Black Like Me,* pp. 223.

107 Griffin warned about saying in a hotel with a strange woman, Bonazzi, *Man in the Mirror,* pp. 147.

107 "...hanged in effigy ...," *Ibid.,* pp. 134.

108 "...settled in a small village ...," *Black Like Me,* pp. 223.

108 "... Mexican communists ...," *Ibid.,* pp. 233.

111 Cyril Connolly quotation, *Man in the Mirror,* pp. 172.

111 "Two American authors ...," Malcolm X. *The Autobiography of Malcolm X.* (New York: Grove Press, 1966), pp. 352-353.

112 "This began as a ...," *Black Like Me,* pp. xi.

112 "His editor at ...," *Man in the Mirror,* pp. 170.

112 October 28 ..., *Black Like Me,* pp. 3.

113 October 29, *Ibid.,* pp. 6.

113 November 7 ..., *Ibid.,* pp. 12.

113   November 8, *Ibid.*, pp. 22.

113   Nov. 10-12, *Ibid.*, pp. 45; Nov. 14, *Ibid.*, pp. 51..

113   "When *Black Like Me* was first published ...," Griffin biographical summary, Columbia University archives.

113   "By the end (of 1961) ...," *Man in the Mirror,* pp. 144-145.

113   "... published in England, France, Germany ...," Griffin biographical summary, Columbia University archives.

115   "He played it angry ...," *Man in the Mirror,* pp. 148.

116   "1,100 lectures ...," *Ibid.*, pp. 149.

116   Klu Klux Klan beating ..., *Ibid.*, pp. 146.

Chapter 9

Page

117   *The John Howard Griffin Reader* ..., biographical summary, Griffin archives, Columbia University.

118   "two glaring weaknesses ...," Bonazzi in *Black Like Me,* pp. 224.

118   "I did not write ...," *Man in the Mirror,* pp. 150.

119   "instead of stimulating any changes ...," *Ibid.*, pp. 150.

119   "almost a command ..." *Ibid.*, pp. 150.

120   "second class Christs ...," Bonazzi, in *Black Like Me,* pp. 225.

120   Newspaper headlines in *Man in the Mirror,* pp. 150-151.

120 "No establishment publisher ...," *Man in the Mirror*, pp. 152.

121 "On Passion Sunday ...," The Church and the Black Man, p. 1.

122 "We have lived under ...," *Ibid.*, pp. 16.

122 "We were told ...," *Ibid.*, pp. 17.

123 "Ten years ago ...," *Ibid.*, pp. 46.

124 "fell on deaf white ears ...," Bonazzi in *Black Like Me*, pp. 229 and "... immediate obscurity," *Man in the Mirror*, pp. 154.

Chapter 10

Page

126 "My first ...," *A Time to Be Human*, pp. 1.

127 "The deepest shock ...," *Ibid.*, pp. 2.

127 "so they could bring in ...," *Ibid.*, pp. 10.

127 "In Nazi Germany ...,' *Ibid.*, pp. 11.

128 Edmund Burke quotations "I know of no way ...," *Ibid.*, pp. 19: "All that is required ...," *Ibid.*, pp. 73.

128 It seems to me, pp. 73

128 "Since segregation was ...," *Ibid.*, pp. 30.

129 "In 1975 ...," *Ibid.*, pp. 37.

130 "What suppressed minorities ...," *Ibid.*, pp. 93.

Chapter 11

Page

131   "Thomas Merton is arguably ...," and "brought about ...," Merton biographical essay, Bellarmine University Library, Louisville, Kentucky.

132   "For his social activism ...," *Ibid.*,

132   Merton wrote seventy books, Merton entry, www.wikipedia.org.

132   List of Merton book titles, Merton biography, Bellarmine University Library.

132   "... the first Cistercian hermit ...," Robert Bonazzi, Foreword, *Follow the Ecstasy,* pp. xii.

133   "The choice was a good one ...," Conger Beasley Jr., Introduction, *The Hermitage Journals,* pp. vi.

133   "Griffin and Merton ...," Robert Bonazzi, Foreword, *Follow the Ecstasy,* pp. ix.

134   "Their work ...'" *Ibid.,* pp. ix.

135   "Merton lived in solitude ...," Griffin, Preface, *The Hermitage Journals*, pp. xv.

135   "5:45 a.m. ...," and "Begin to read the Asian journal ...," *Ibid.,* pp. 1, 2.

136   "Then I read ..., *Ibid.,* pp. 3.

136   "The sense of loneliness ...,' *Ibid.,* pp. 13.

137   "Since the days ...," *Ibid.,* pp. 23.

138   "I am preoccupied ...," *Ibid.,* pp. 24.

138   "I am terribly preoccupied ...," *Ibid.,* pp. 27-28.

139   Benign foot tumors ..., e-mail from Robert Bonazzi to author, June 1, 2010.

139 "Now I have to get up ...," *The Hermitage Journals,* pp. 33.

139 "Brother Patrick found ...," *Ibid.,* pp. 34-35.

140 "I am aware ...," *Ibid.,* pp. 40.

140 "It is the happiest ...," *Ibid.,* pp. 44.

140 "Cannot resist ...," *Ibid.,* pp. 55-56.

140 "Back in the hermitage ...," *Ibid.,* pp. 79.

141 "But I ache all over ...," *Ibid.,* pp. 103.

141 "Went to Connecticut ...,' *Ibid.,* pp. 104.

142 "Turned on the weather ...," *Ibid.,* pp. 111.

143 "Now I hear the truck ...,' *Ibid.,* pp. 117-118.

144 "Fascinating, in a way ...," *Ibid.,* 120-121.

144 "While shaving ...," *Ibid.,* pp. 132.

145 "I feel utterly unequal ...," *Ibid.,* pp. 133..

146 "Brother Patrick ...," *Ibid.,* pp. 141-142

146 "Again, I note ...," *Ibid.,* pp. 146.

148 "Have heard that ...'" *Ibid.,* pp. 164. The reference to "Dan" was Daniel Berrigan, brother of Philip Berrigan. Both were Catholic priests and considered radicals. Both Berrigan brothers were, for a time, on the FBI Ten Most Wanted Fugitives list for committing acts of vandalism including destroying government property: www.wikipedai.org.

148 "It was one of the most moving hours ...," *Ibid.,* pp. 185.

149 "Today is the ...," *Ibid.,* pp. 193.

149 "Lord, I see and hear ...," *Ibid.,* pp. 208.

150 "I feel a profound sense ...,' *Ibid.,* pp. 231.

Chapter 12

Chapter 13

173   Father Tom McKillop and Luiz de Moura-Castro, Robert Bonazzi e-mail to author, June 7, 2010.

178   Elisabeth Kübler-Ross profile, www.wikipedia.org.

186   "He died of everything ...," quoted in Bonazzi, *Man in the Mirror,* pp. 168.

Complete Works of John Howard Griffin

Books

1952   **The Devil Rides Outside**, novel.

first edition, cloth, Smiths Inc., Fort Worth, 596 pp.

1953   British edition, cloth, William Collins, London & Glasgow, 511 pp.

French edition, cloth, Presses de la Cite, Paris, 458 pp. Translated by H. de Sarbois.

1954   paperback edition, Pocket Books, New York, 579 pp.

Dutch edition, cloth, Elsevier, Amsterdam & Brussels. 492 pp. Translated by J. W. Hofstra.

1956   **Nuni**, novel.

Houghton Mifflin, Boston, 310 pp. first edition, cloth,

British edition, cloth, The Riverside Press, Cambridge, 310 pp.

1958   German edition, cloth, Schunemann,
        Bremen, 303 pp.

        Translated by Helmut and Christel
        Wiemken.

1959   **The Land of the High Sky,** nonfiction.

        First edition, cloth, The First National Bank
        of Midland, 212 pp.

1961   **Black Like Me**, First edition, cloth,
        Houghton Mifflin, 176 pp.

1962   Signet paperback edition, New American
        Library, New York.

        Canadian edition, cloth, Thomas Allen,
        Toronto.

        British edition, cloth, William Collins Ltd.
        London & Glasgow.

        French edition, paperback, Gallimard,
        Paris. Translated by Marguerite de
        Gramont.

        Polish edition, paperback, Isicry, Warsaw.
        Translated by Josef Giebultowicz.

1963   Dutch edition cloth, Wereldbibliotheek,
        Amsterdam. Translated by H. vanTeylinger.

        Italian edition, paperback, Longanesi.
        Translated by Elisa Morpurgo.

Portuguese edition, paperback Publaicacoes Europa-America Ltd. Lisbon & Rio de Janero. Translated by Raul Correia.

1964   Norwegian edition, cloth, Ernst G. Mortensen, Olso. Translated by Elmar T. Schoning.

1965   British paperback edition, Grafton, London. Dutch paperback edition, Wereldbibliotheek, Amsterdam.

1966   Hungarian edition, paperback, Mora Ferenc, Budapest. Translated by Takas Zoltan.

1967   Japanese cloth edition, Chikum Shobo Ltd., Toyko.
Boxed set with *The Roses of Dallas*, on JFK assassination.
Japanese paperback ed., Charles Tuttle/ Shiseido, Toyko. Translated by Isao Sekiguchi.
Braille edition, Wellington Braille Club (via Wm Collins Ltd.).

1968   Danish edition, paperback, Winther's Forlag, Copenhagen. (no translation credit).

Swedish edition, paperback, Raben &
Sjorgren, Stockholm. Translated by Jan
Sjogren.
Norwegian paperback edition, Mortensen,
Oslo.

1976   Chechoslovakian edition, paperback, Mlada
Fronta, Prague. Translated by Pavel Sar.

1976   **Black Like Me**, second edition, with
Epilogue by John Howard Griffin. Houghton
Mifflin, Boston,. 208 pp.

1977   second edition, Signet Paperback, New
American Library, New York. 188 pp.

1987   second edition, Signet Paperback library,
NAL/Penguin, New York.

1996   35th Anniversary Edition, Signet
Paperback Penguin, New York. 192 pp.

2001   Limited Edition hardback, 750, Buccaneer
Books, Inc., Long Island, NY.

2003   Trade paperback edition, New American
Library, New York. 200 pp.

2004   Audio Book (CD and cassette) Audio
Bookshelf, Northpoint, Maine.

2004   Griffin Estate Edition, Wings Press, San Antonio. 239 pp.

2006   Revised Griffin Estate Edition (with first Index),
Wings Press. 243 pp.

2006   Japanese Translation, Blues Interactions via Tuttle-Mori Agency Inc., Toyko.

2009   German edition in English, Diesterweg, Edited and annotated by Rudolph F. Rau.

2009   United Kingdom Edition, Souvenir Press, London.

1968   **The John Howard Griffin Reader**
Edited by Bradford Daniel; Introduction by Maxwell Geismar. First edition, cloth, Houghton Mifflin. 588 pp.

1969   **The Church and the Black Man**
Text and photographs by Griffin and others. Pflaum Press, Dayton. 132 pp.

1970   French paperback edition, Desclee de Brouwer, Paris.

1970   **A Hidden Wholeness: The Visual World of Thomas Merton**

Text, photographs and artwork by John Howard Griffin. First edition, cloth, Houghton Mifflin, 146 pp.

1977   Cloth reprint, Norman S. Berg Co., Dunwoody, Ga.

1973   **Twelve Photographic Portraits**
Cloth and paperback editions, Unicorn Press, Greensboro, N.C.

1974   **Jacques Maritain: Homage in Words and Pictures**
Cloth, Magi Books, Albany, N.Y.
1981   Italian cloth edition, Editrice Massimo, Milan.

1977   **A Time To Be Human**
First cloth edition, Macmillan, New York & Toronto.
Cloth edition, Collier-Macmillan, London (simutaneous publication)

1981   **The Hermitage Journals:**
A Diary Kept While Working on the Biography of Thomas Merton
First edition cloth, Andrews & McMeel, Kansas City.

1983   Doubleday Image paperback edition, New
        York.

1983   **Follow the Ecstasy:**
        Thomas Merton, The Hermitage Years,
        1965–1968
        First edition trade paperback, Latitudes
        Press, Fort Worth.

1993   **Follow the Ecstasy:**
        The Hermitage Years of Thomas Merton
        Revised edition, trade paperback, Orbis
        Books, Maryknoll, N.Y.

1993   British trade paperback edition, Burns &
        Oates, London.

1997   German trade paperback edition, Vier-
        Turme-Verlag, Munich.

1985   **Pilgrimage**
        Short story, limited edition chapbook,
        Latitudes Press,
        Fort Worth.

1997   **Encounters with the Other: A Personal**
        Journey
        Trade paperback, Latitudes Press, Fort
        Worth.

2003   **Street of the Seven Angels**
Novel, first edition cloth, Wings Press, San
Antonio.

2007   **Available Light: Exile In Mexico**
Photographs. First edition with French
flaps, Wings Press, San Antonio.

Monographs

1939   *Interpretation of the Ornaments of the
Music for Keyboard Instruments of the 17th
and 18th Centuries.*
Co-author, Father Pierre Froger. Cathedral
of Tours, limited edition.

1949   *Handbook for Darkness: a Guide for the
Sighted.*
American Foundation for the Blind.

1956   *What Happened in Mansfield: A Report of
the Crisis*
*Situation Resulting from Efforts to
Desegregate the*
School System. Co-author, Theodore
Freedman.
Anti-Defamation League of B'nai Brith, New
York.

1962   *The Cultivated Mind*
Guardian Genius of Democracy:
The Contributions of Religious Institutions
to Higher Education in Texas, 1689-1962.
University of Dallas, Irving, Tx.

1962   *The Singing Boys of Mexico.*
Mexico City, DF.

1963   *Racist Sins of Christians.*
Passionist Missions, Union City, N,.J.
(reprinted in **The John Howard Griffin Reader**.)

1969   *On Our Doorstep.*
Pio Decimo Press, St. Louis.

1969   *Racial Equality: The Myth and the Reality.*
University of Iowa, Iowa City.
Microfiche, Columbia University, 1979.

1970   *The Thomas Merton Studies Center.*
cloth and paper editions, Unicorn Press,
Greensboro, N.C.

Supplemental Readings

Baldwin, James. *The Fire Next Time*. New York: The Dial Press, 1963.

Bonazzi, Robert. *Man in the Mirror: John Howard Griffin and the Story of Black Like Me*. Maryknoll, New York: Orbis Books, 1997.

Boyle, Sarah Patton. *The Desegregated Heart*. New York: William Morrow, 1962.

East, P.D. *The Magnolia Jungle: The Life, Times and Education of a Southern Editor*. New York: Simon and Schuster, 1960.

Fensch, Thomas. *Steinbeck and Covici: The Story of a Friendship*. Middlebury, Vt.: Paul S. Eriksson, Publisher, 1979.

Halsell, Grace. *Soul Sister*. New York: World Publishing Co., 1969.

King, Martin Luther, Jr. *Why We Can't Wait*. New York: Harper & Row, 1964.

Kubler-Ross, Elisabeth. *On Death and Dying*. New York: Macmillan, 1969.

Loeb, Paul Rogat. *Soul of a Citizen: Living with Conviction in Challenging Times*. New York: St. Martin's Press, 2010.

McKillop, Thomas. *Friendship and Second Innocence: Two Souls in Conversation*. Montreal: Novalis Publishing, 2008.

Myrdal, Gunnar. *An American Dilemma: The Negro Problem and Modern Democracy*. New York: Harper & Row, 1944.

Smith, Lillian. *Killers of the Dream*. New York: W.W. Norton Co., 1978.

Sprigle, Ray. *In the Land of Jim Crow*. New York: Simon & Schuster, 1949.

Steinbeck, John. *The Grapes of Wrath*. New York: The Viking Press, 1939.

Terkel, Studs. *American Dreams: Lost and Found*. New York: Pantheon Books, 1980.

Wald, Gayle. *Crossing the Line: Racial Passing in Twentieth-century U.S. Literature and Culture*. Durham, N.C.: Duke University Press, 2000.

Index

About the author ...

Thomas Fensch has published two previous books in his "The Man Who..." series: *The Man Who Was Dr. Seuss: The Life and Work of Theodor Geisel* and *The Man Who Was Walter Mitty: The Life and Work of James Thurber*.

He has published four books about John Steinbeck; two about James Thurber; two about Theodor "Dr. Seuss" Geisel; one each on Oskar Schindler and Ernest Hemingway; one memoir and other nonfiction titles. He has an international reputation in John Steinbeck criticism. *Steinbeck and Covici: The Story of a Friendship* is generally considered one of the seminal books in Steinbeck scholarship.

He has a doctorate from Syracuse University, is a member of the faculty of Virginia Union University, Richmond and lives in Ashland, Virginia.

www.ingramcontent.com/pod-product-compliance
Lightning Source LLC
Chambersburg PA
CBHW020244290326
41930CB00038B/236